THE DIVORCED DAD'S HANDBOOK

If you want to know how . . .

Writing an Assignment
Proven techniques from a chief examiner that really gets results

Writing an Essay
Simple techniques to transform your coursework and examinations

Critical Thinking for Students
Learn the skills of critical assessment and effective argument

Writing Your Dissertation
How to plan, prepare and present successful work

Returning to Learning
A practical handbook for adults returning to education

howtobooks

For full details, please send for a free copy
of the latest catalogue to:

How To Books
Spring Hill House, Spring Hill Road, Begbroke
Oxford OX5 1RX, United Kingdom
email: info@howtobooks.co.uk
www.howtobooks.co.uk

THE DIVORCED DAD'S HANDBOOK

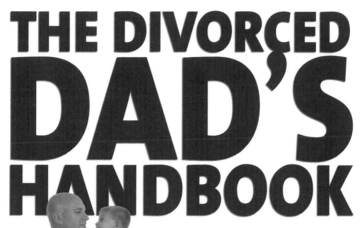

ADVICE, SUPPORT
AND GUIDANCE
FOR ALL FATHERS
GOING TROUGH
SEPARATION OR
DIVORCE

STEVE DAVIES

howtobooks

First published by How To Books Ltd,
Spring Hill House, Spring Hill Road,
Begbroke, Oxford OX5 1RX, United Kingdom.
Tel: (01865) 375794. Fax: (01865) 379162.
email: info@howtobooks.co.uk
www.howtobooks.co.uk

British Library Cataloguing in Publication Data.
A catalogue record for this book is available from the British Library.

ISBN: 978 1 84528 147 2

Cover design by Baseline Arts Ltd, Oxford
Produced for How To Books by Deer Park Productions, Tavistock
Typeset by Kestrel Data, Exeter, Devon
Printed and bound by Bell & Bain Ltd, Glasgow

NOTE: The material contained in this book is set out in good faith for general
guidance and no liability can be accepted for loss or expense incurred as a result of
relying in particular circumstances on statements made in the book. Laws and
regulations are complex and liable to change, and readers should check the
current position with the relevant authorities before making personal
arrangements.

Contents

List of case studies

Acknowledgements

I wish to thank all the divorced dads who contributed to this book by sharing with me their experiences and insights into the many issues that they faced.

I wish them all well in their continuing journeys as divorced dads.

Steve Davies

Introduction

40 per cent of all fathers lose contact with their children within two years.

Dame Elizabeth Butler-Sloss

100 children a day lose partial or total contact with their fathers in the UK.

Figures from the Lord Chancellor's Department

The first few weeks of being separated can be, both practically and emotionally, the worst time of a divorced dad's new life. It would be great to say that life will improve. However, whilst you may come to terms emotionally with the changes in your relationship with your children, many other obstacles lie in the way of a straightforward and fulfilling relationship with them. Not all fathers make that journey – which is why up to 100 children a day in the UK lose partial or total contact with their fathers. Each divorced dad has to decide if he will remain in contact with his children – or whether he will be one of the thousands of dads in the UK who does not. Unfortunately that decision may not be his alone to make.

The problem is simple, and needs to be stated clearly. The law, the court system and pretty much all the other aspects of a divorced dad's life are heavily weighted against him. If you are a dad who has just been through a separation, and you believe that your and your children's rights will prevail, then you need to think again and start to understand your position.

There are things you should know and tips that will help you be a successful divorced dad. They will also stop you from making mistakes that will cost you dearly – not just financially but in the relationship you have, and want, with your children. As one divorced dad I know said, 'It's not about winning, it's about the degree of losing.'

The most important thing in your life is, of course, your children. Ensuring that you can create the space and time to build on the relationship that you already have with them is a major goal. The chances are that this was the case when you lived in the marital home, but now that your status has changed, you will also need to change the way you handle your relationships with your children.

The sad fact is that, instead of seeing his kids more or less every day, the average divorced dad now sees his children less than once a week. A recent study by the Department for Constitutional Affairs (DfCA) (Alison Blackwell et al) found that,

> *Overall, at least half of all children had some form of contact (direct or indirect contact) with their non-resident parent at least once a week: and that . . . fewer than three in ten children stayed over night with their non-resident parent at least once a week.*
> Non-resident Parent Contact Report (DfCA Oct 2003)

What this study shows is that almost half the children involved in a break up in the UK lose the input of their dad in their daily lives. This is a staggering statistic. The study also reported that up to 70 per cent of children stay overnight less than once a week with their fathers. This is a very revealing statistic which shows just how minimal the level of contact that the children have with their fathers can become.

Of course, there are many reasons for this lack of contact. Sometimes it is because the father himself does not wish to continue to have a relationship with his children, but in a lot of cases this is not so.

The study also reports that over the first few years of separation there is a massive reduction in the number of children who have contact from their dads – from 84 per cent in the first two years to 53 per cent in the fourth year. Among children in the non-resident parent sample just over a half (53 per cent) of those whose parents had been separated for at least three years had direct contact with their non-resident parent at least once a week compared with around four-fifths of children whose parents had separated more recently (79 per cent of children whose parents separated less than a year ago, 84 per cent of children whose parents separated one year but less than two years ago).

This means that there are up to a hundred children a day, or thousands of children per year, losing contact with their fathers. The reasons are complicated, but for many divorced dads the struggle to keep up the relationship in the face of a legal system that does not give the father any useful rights is simply too overwhelming.

This book is designed to help fathers continue with that struggle so that dads, and more importantly their children, can benefit from having a sustained and loving relationship. Studies by psychologists over the last 25 years have proved that having a balanced relationship with two parents – even if one is a non-resident father – is better for the children than being brought up with the influence of just one parent.

Good luck in that struggle. I hope this book will help fathers to understand the environment that they are in, and how best to cope.

Steve Davies

1

Separation

THE FIRST FEW MONTHS

To your child, the separation of their parents is, of course, a major change in their lives. Depending on the ages of the children, the way in which they will react to your separation will vary. The best news here is that children can actually be emotionally stronger than adults, and they frequently react better to major changes in their routine than adults do.

The age of the child is important in a separation for several reasons. Their level of understanding about what is going on changes depending on their age. And, just as importantly, the older the child the stronger your relationship will be. Also – and this is a bit more subtle – the older the child, the more likely it is that the contact arrangements will be made informally with them, rather than having to get agreement with the ex-partner for access.

Over two in five children (42 per cent) aged 11 to 16 years had their arrangements informally agreed between their parents compared with 55 per cent of children aged under 11 years.

Non-resident Parent Contact Report (DfCA Oct 2003)

Being able to make contact arrangements informally (ie without the need for a solicitor or the intervention of the courts) is a key factor in the nature of the relationship that many divorced dads will have with their children. Many divorced dads report that as their children grow up, and they are able to agree contact and access directly with them, the stress and other problems related to having to negotiate with their ex-partner is completely removed. Many barriers to developing that relationship disappear, which enhances the father–child relationship for both parties. Children's understanding of what is going on is also affected by other factors. If they are at school, then they will be mixing with other kids whose parents are separated, and pick up what is going on from them. Also, if your children are of different age groups (which is typical in a family) then they will talk amongst themselves and learn from each other.

It is important to ensure that the way you communicate matches your children's age and understanding. What every divorced dad needs to realise very quickly is that a change has taken place and that needs a change in attitude from both himself and his children. Many doubts will creep into the divorced dad's head, and many obstacles will have to be overcome if he is to remain a long-term influence in his child's life.

Yet you will still have a relationship with your kids, unless you choose not to. Unfortunately the statistics are clear on this subject: in excess of 40 per cent of dads lose contact with their kids. It is up to each divorced dad to what he wants to do.

TIP

Your relationship with your child is for *you* to determine. What you need to do now is concentrate on that, not on the separation or the divorce.

This is the first tip in this book, and is by far the most important of them all. The time that you have already invested in your children's lives – all the normal family duties – will be wasted and your relationship ruined if you fail to focus your efforts on them. You must maintain your focus on their needs rather than on your own (at least during the time that you spend with your children).

For example, children hate to see either parent sniping at the other, or being hurt by the other. If this happens it could have a detrimental long-term emotional effect on the child. Even in very difficult circumstances, you need to strive at all times to make your time with the kids a positive one. You may need, for example, to keep up the illusion, however difficult, that your attitude towards their mother is positive, or at worst neutral – irrespective of what she has done to you.

Even if your ex has initiated the separation and you are hurt and angry, you must avoid expressing these feelings in front of the children. It might make you feel better but it will leave the children feeling anxious and confused because they love you both.

So the first thing that any divorced dad needs to do is to look forward, to realise that his, and his children's, world has changed, and to get on with reacting as positively as he can to that change.

Your child's emotions in the first few months

Whilst you will be going through your own emotional journey, your child will be too, and a great dad should have an awareness of what they are going through. But unless your parents got divorced when you were a child and so you have been there yourself, it is unlikely that you will know what it's like.

All children are different, and their emotional journey will be a difficult one. As a divorced dad you can help that journey by taking time out to think about what your child is going through. How you communicate with them will vary depending, for example, if you have a teenager who is capable of understanding the separation, or a two year old who has no idea of what is going on.

One thing that you need to think hard about is what memories your child will have of this time in their lives. Do you want them to remember this period as one where there was major conflict, anger and even violence in their family? Or would you prefer them to have as smooth a transition as possible? Your actions and efforts can have a big impact on how they remember this time, and how they are affected by it.

In the first few weeks of separation try to focus on your immediate needs and the needs of your children. Avoid planning new activities or other changes. Over time there will be opportunities for you to grow and change, but during the first few weeks of a separation your kids will need to see you as much as you can. They will be dealing with all the different emotions that this situation brings. Even though it may be tough facing your ex-partner during this period, and many divorced dads have to eat large helpings of humble pie for no good reason, try and make contact during this period several times a week. Your kids need to know that you are still around and that it is important to you that you are a part of their lives.

Access problems

Unfortunately, many separations are not amicable and the resident parent (normally the mother) will from the outset control the amount of time that you can spend with your kids. It is not uncommon for a mother to stop access as a way of hurting the father during the first few weeks. If this happens to you then you are one of many, many dads who are faced with this issue.

The bad news is that there is not much you can do about it, and at a time when you and your kids need contact most, that contact can often be thwarted for no good reason other than emotional hurt from an ex-partner. But don't panic, and don't make mistakes that will come back to haunt you. Don't make scenes, and be angry with your ex. You *will* get access if you are the legal father. The best thing to do is not to create reasons for this period to be longer than it needs to be.

If access is stopped in the first few weeks:

- **Never abuse or hurt** your ex-partner or any others. Assault can, and will, be used in the future to stop access. This abuse includes both physical and verbal.

- **Record what happens**. Get a diary and record times and dates when access was refused. This will be a critical piece of evidence if you need to apply for a court order for access later in the process.

- **Avoid shouting** or slanging matches with your ex. It achieves nothing other than to provide entertainment for the neighbours, and if overheard by the kids is detrimental to their relationship with you.

- **Don't try and take your kids** from school or any other place without the knowledge and consent of mum.

- **Explain to your kids**, when you finally see them, that you want to see them and that you are sorting out the problems.

- **Email your child** if they are old enough. Often email is a great communication tool, which the ex-partner normally cannot influence.

- **Relax . . .** because you *will* get access. Even an ex-partner who at this stage is being completely unreasonable will eventually have to succumb to the rights of the child to see both parents. So try and keep stress levels low.

- **Use a mobile phone.** If your child is old enough to use a mobile, buy them one as a method of direct communication.

- **Talk to your family** or to other divorced dads – they will be able to help you understand what is going on, and help you to deal with the stress of the situation.

- **Recognise** that this will be a stressful time. Find ways to deal with that stress.

It may be that stopping your access to the kids is just an initial reaction by your ex to the separation which gets sorted out quickly. If it persists then you will need to take action in order to get time with the kids. However, if you and your partner are splitting up fairly amicably or you are attempting to agree on issues over the kids, then try to discuss before you leave the family home what the arrangements over access and contact for the children is going to be.

Prior to your separation, seek out and, if you can, write up a simple agreement. You might feel that this is not necessary, but to introduce a written plan as a way of ensuring that you both understand the arrangements, is a good idea. It is likely that at this stage of your separation-communication is, or will be, a major problem; introduce a written document as an informal thing – you can tell her that you are just trying to put your thoughts on paper and ask her if she agrees with what you're thinking.

The first few months – financially

With the average household in the UK having debts of over £7,700 (see www.creditaction.org.uk), it is probable that you don't have a stack of cash put by for rainy days. Over the next few months demands for money will come from unexpected sources so the first few months of a separation is likely to be a very stressful time for your wallet. You may need cash to pay for a deposit for a new place to live, money to pay rent and other bills that will be added to your outgoings. At the same time the amount of money in your pocket is likely to decrease because you will need to pay some interim maintenance payments for the children.

It will probably be several months, if not a year or so, until you can put your finances in order. You may have to wait for the outcome of your financial settlement (if there were assets) in your divorce.

You need to go through a budgeting process straight away to ensure that you do not slip into further debt and can afford the new expenses in your life:

◆ **Go and see your bank manager:** tell him about your separation, especially if you need short-term financial help.

◆ **Ensure that you are not liable** for any of your ex-partner's ongoing finances.

◆ **Minimise your expenditure** until you have completed a budgeting process for yourself.

◆ **Let your employer know** (via the HR dept) what is happening; you may need some time off at short notice to go to meetings or deal with a problem.

◆ **Change your bank account:** ensure that your ex-partner does not have access to your current money.

◆ **Open a new account** if you think that your ex-partner will come after you for more cash than you are prepared to give. If you have to, get a friend to do it in their name. Put any cash you get into it so she cannot trace it back to you (for example bonuses at work or cash from selling assets such as a car, etc).

◆ **If you have any savings** make sure that you are in control of them, and that your ex-partner cannot spend them as she wants (she will always come up with an excuse later if it is contested).

◆ **If you change jobs and/or get a pay rise**, you may wish to keep it close to your chest.

CASE STUDY

Dealing with the first few months
Dad: Lee
Children: Sophie and Jacob
Situation: Divorced in 2000

My separation was not what I wanted; my wife had an affair. One day, she simply sat me down and told me that she wanted to leave, and then about four weeks later she and the children left.

The day we told the kids was the worst day of my life. We sat them down in the kitchen and told them that mummy and daddy were no longer going to live together and that they would be moving to a new home. Both kids burst into tears, and so did we.

The day they moved out I went to work, and when I got home much of the furniture was gone, and there was emptiness. I just slumped down in the corner of the room in silence. For me it was terrible: all my aspirations of bringing up my children in a two-parent family (which I never had) were blown away. I knew that I would feel low, but in truth I reckon I suffered from depression for at least the first six months, if not longer.

My ex was, and still is, a good mum, and the kids were very close to her, so it was natural that they both went to live with her. In fact when I asked my solicitor about residency he told me that unless I could prove that she was an alcoholic, or a druggie, then my chances of getting residence were virtually nil, so it was not an issue that I could have any say over.

Most divorced dads miss the daily routine of seeing and interacting with their children, and this becomes a great source of sorrow. They miss the chance to read a bedtime story, or have daily meals with the kids, and are not there when their child falls off the swing in the garden, or to help with homework. If you are a typical divorced dad then you will feel the same way.

Missing out on the daily routine is one of the hardest parts of being a divorced dad. Recognise that you share this feeling with almost every man in your situation and develop strategies to cope with it:

◆ If you find yourself slipping into a depression because it is ten at night and you have not had contact with your kids, turn your negative emotion into a positive one by planning what you will do with them when you can next see them. Focus on what you will do next: visualise the moment, and look forward to it.

◆ Talk to a friend. Or even better . . .

◆ Talk to your mum. You may be surprised that your mum is probably the best listener that you can turn to. She will know what you are feeling and will not make judgements about your emotions.

Or you could go down the pub, get drunk with your mates and feel even worse the next day.

The fact of the matter is that this new routine is a part of your new life. Unless you are planning to get back together with your ex this is a part of your future that you will have to come to terms with. It's a fact in your change of role as a divorced dad.

There are other negative aspects about your new role as a divorced dad. If you want to get depressed about it the list is endless: schooling, hobbies, what they can watch on TV, how much TV they can watch and so on . . . your influence in these areas will now be small. But you need to focus on what you *can* achieve and how you can influence the upbringing of your children, not on what you can't control. Focusing on the negatives will make you depressed, angry and bitter; this will add to your stress levels and affect your outlook on your current position.

The fact that you are not there for much of it does not mean that you need to remove yourself from whole aspects of your child's life. In fact it is important for the development of your child that they know that you are taking an interest in all the events in their lives. Make sure that you become aware of what is going on in your child's environment outside the home.

Just because you are not around all the time, don't remove yourself from other aspects of your child's life. Continue to take an active interest in, and be concerned about:

- school
- friends
- homework
- TV
- hobbies
- sport.

Your child will also want to know that you are still interested and want to share their successes and failings with you in these areas. Try to be around and take an interest as they will want to share these things with you. This will be very difficult in the early stages

Before starting to consider your parenting plan, you need to agree some access/contact arrangements with your ex-partner. Hopefully this can be done in the early stage of your separation, on an informal basis. This may be a source of difficulty that you will need to go to the family court to resolve (this is covered in more detail in Chapter 3). Don't worry if, initially, your ex does not allow you the access that you want, and don't worry if for the first few months of your separation it seems as if your children are mixed up about your new situation. Things should calm down a bit later.

The important view is medium to long term. You have already made the decision to remain an active dad, so now it is time to consider what that will actually mean, given the change in your circumstances.

Making arrangements

There is no need to create a complex and detailed plan of action. In the short term you need to think about the following questions:

- When will I see my children?

- How long will I see them for?

- What will I do with them in the time that I have?

- What will I tell them about the separation?

- What help do I need with my contact?

- What other relations (grandparents and so on) do the children still want to see?

- What will the living arrangements be in the early days before I have a long-term home?

◆ Who will continue the child's religious education (if any)?

◆ What arrangements will we have for special days?

◆ What holidays can the children come on with me?

There will be a hundred and one different aspects to the arrangements for your children. Don't expect to know all the answers when you first separate from your ex-partner; the arrangements will have to develop and change over time. What you need to do is to ensure that you have thought through the basics. That way you can create time and space for good contact with your children; this will cater for their needs as well as being practical for you and your ex-partner. It may mean that you have to be more flexible than you would want to be in the first few months, just to establish a good working relationship with your ex-partner.

It cannot be stressed strongly enough at this stage that, if you can create an informal working relationship with your ex-partner, it will benefit the children immensely. It doesn't just show them that there is minimal stress between their parents, but also in the longer term it will help you to have more time with your children.

When can I see the children?

There is no formula for telling you when, where and for how long to see your kids. There is no manual written for being a parent – it is not a subject studied at school, nor is parenting an exact science. In the initial stages of the separation it is excellent to see the children as much as possible, but work and other life commitments will soon mean that a routine will be needed.

Most children like routine, and it is critical that they know when they will be seeing you (managing contact is covered in

Chapter 2), so establishing a routine is important. This is especially true for children under the age of 10. Not only is it important for the children but it is also important for you, as you will need to plan your life around the time with your kids. As your children become young adults, so contact times will need to be more flexible, and will probably be based around the child's activities – rather than when you are available to see them. Try telling a teenager that they can't go to a sleepover at their best friend's because you want to see them. The older they get the more flexible you need to be.

In the initial stages of your parenting plan, consider only your child's needs – you can catch up on your social life later. If it means that you don't play football on a Sunday morning because this is the only time that your children are available, then hand your temporary resignation into the football club and tell them you will be back later.

As time goes by it will be necessary for you to balance your life, to create time for your children as well as having time to develop your own interests. And if you are lucky, you can share a lot of those interests with your children. Don't make the mistake of creating a parenting plan that does not allow you to grow as a person and have your own interests. You are a person as well as a dad; even though your kids are an important part of your life, they are not its sole purpose.

TIP

In the first year of your separation try and put the children first; they will need you at this time more than ever.

Your ex-partner

Some women will want their ex to have as much access as possible, to allow them to develop their own lives. One of the reasons that some women wanted a divorce in the first place was because they felt they were trapped. So there may be a tendency for your ex to manipulate contact arrangements around what time/days are suitable for her.

That is not the way that contact should be arranged. Contact should be designed around the needs of the child. But in the initial stages of the parenting plan, adapting to your ex might be the best solution to gaining unencumbered access to your children.

Don't be a babysitter for your ex-partner's benefit. Design your contact times around the needs of the children.

◆ If your ex is more likely to give you access to suit her, then initially you may have to accept it. There's no problem, if you get to spend time with the kids. But that does not mean that you have to accept it as a permanent arrangement.

◆ Keep a record of times that you spend with the kids in the early months; it can be great evidence if you need to go to court for access rights. If you are being used, you will be able to prove that the times that your ex-partner is giving you are not in the best interests of the kids.

◆ If you have to, refuse any arrangements that are not suitable for you. Be prepared to be flexible, but don't be a babysitting service. If you have to refuse, suggest alternatives rather than simply saying no again. Document the alternatives that you give.

◆ Try to talk to your ex-partner and discuss the needs of the children, especially if they are under five. Your ex-partner will probably want reassuring that the child's needs are being met.

A good way of working out what to do in the first few months is to talk to other divorced dads who have been in this situation before you. Try to learn from what mistakes they have made, so that you can avoid the errors yourself. If you do talk to other divorced dads you will probably find that the following times are a good contact arrangement for the initial period.

Child's age	Times per week	Hours of contact	Stay over
0–1	3	2	0
2–4	2	3	2
5–9	2	5	1
10–13	2	10	2
13–16+		The child can decide	

However, don't get concerned if your ex-partner will not give you as much time as in the table above. You may not be in a position to negotiate better terms, but hopefully that will change at a later date.

How long should I see the children for?

Let's get one thing straight: quality not quantity is the important thing. This is why many divorced dads have an excellent relationship with their kids, even if they cannot see them every day. This is because of a change in the balance of activities during the time that you have access to them. You can devote 100 per cent of your attention to them. Think back to when you were at home. How often did you have the option of devoting several hours purely to the children, unencumbered by domestic chores?

So if you want to be a positive influence on your child, then it is the quality of your contact that will count, not the quantity. But clearly there must be a base level for involvement with a child's life – just a few hours each month is not enough. You need to establish weekly contact at least. How much depends on your child's age, but for children of all ages contact can be in two ways. Indirect contact, such as phone calls or emails, is just as important as direct contact – seeing them. Every divorced dad needs to strive to have both indirect and direct contact with his children. Obviously, indirect contact is more important if the father is unable to have direct contact each week.

TIP

Every child is different so there is no set formula. You must endeavour to have both direct and indirect contact based on what you believe to be the needs of *your* child.

Contact should also include both daytime and stay-over arrangements, and it is preferable in your initial parenting plan to establish a routine that includes both. However this may not be possible if your new domestic arrangement is a bedsit in nowhere land, and you can't bring yourself to show your kids your new surroundings.

From the start, your contact should include both daytime and stay-over arrangements.

◆ If your accommodation is not up to much at first then use alternatives which the children may already be familiar with, such as grandparents' or other relatives' homes.

◆ Children's memories of you will be formed at this time – so think about the impression that your child will take from you at this time.

◆ When looking for your new home, think about the needs of your children (if your finances allow).

◆ Don't take the kids round to your new partner's house straight away (if you have one). You may well find your cat in a saucepan boiling away on the stove the next time you go home. Your ex-partner will not want you playing happy families in the initial period of your separation.

◆ Try to ensure that your contact works around the normal routine of the children, rather than them having to change.

What shall I do when I'm with them?

In the first few weeks, your kids don't need to do activities that you don't normally do with them. Just seeing you and spending time with you is probably what they need. You need to give them time to talk to you – not to spend time on funfair rides or expensive trips. In the first few weeks try to think more about what your kids are going through than you. This initial period is important. You need to ensure that you don't add to the fears and woes of your kids and, if you are having problems, seek to assure them that things will become OK after a short period.

TIP

Don't be too ambitious at first. The key is to consider what your children's needs are.

It's a good idea to write it down. Somehow, writing something makes you think about it a great deal more. You don't need a fancy computer, just a blank sheet of paper which says: 'What do my children need over the next few months?'

Somewhere on that piece of paper may be written love, security and encouragement, along with knowing that you will always be around. There will no doubt be many others things but I doubt that anywhere will be written new toys, day trips to Alton Towers, fancy holidays or other special treats. You don't have to go spending money on your kids to compensate for your change in circumstances: it is not what they need, nor will doing those things build your relationship long term with your children.

Many children will wonder if your divorce will mean changes in their lives. For example, if you used to take them to the local sports club, they will be thinking, will they still be able to go now that you are not at home? Or if they had some pocket money from you . . . will they still get it?

It is quite natural for them to be negative in their outlook, to worry about the small things, and of course to think the worse. Your role is simple: talk to your children if they are old enough to express their views, and reassure them as much as possible.

Talk to your children. They are the best source of feedback that you can have.

◆ When you talk to them, don't make it a formal chat. Do it as casually as you can, maybe whilst playing in the park.

◆ The more relaxed you can make your children, the more communicative they will be.

◆ Concentrate on discovering what their needs are.

◆ Where possible focus on their fears and worries, and address them.

◆ If your child is under 10, then you will need to adopt a different strategy as they may not be able to communicate clearly what is going on in their heads.

◆ Don't discuss with them your fears or worries – your job as a parent is to shoulder those.

◆ Reassure and encourage your children at every opportunity.

◆ Don't make any promises that you know you can't keep absolutely. Your children will remember if you let them down and it will come back to haunt you.

When you have your children, don't just sit them down in front of the TV – plan some activities. These do not have to cost you any money. In terms of the activities you can do, try to plan things that you can do together: swimming, walking, playing in the park or board games at home. Now is the time to get out the Christmas present that Auntie Jane gave your child, the one that has been gathering dust because you did not have the time to play that game with your children before.

All your kids will want in the early stages is to spend time with you. Playing games is the best way for kids to have fun, and you will get a great deal of satisfaction from seeing the smiles on their faces when they beat you at Snakes and Ladders or Mousetrap, Monopoly or Draughts. What's more, you probably don't need to buy them, as they'll already be somewhere in your kid's bedroom.

Simply spending quality time together is about focusing on your child's emotional and educational needs; it is not about being a Disneyland dad. In your initial parenting plan, focus on simply spending energy on your kids, not money.

TELLING YOUR CHILDREN ABOUT THE SEPARATION

What exactly you tell your children will be affected by how old they are, and also the reason for your separation. Once your kids are teenagers, they will probably already know what is going on. They are very sensitive to the dynamics within their own home and it will come as no great surprise that you or mum are leaving. So there is probably not so much to say to this age group – you will need to focus on the ongoing arrangements and continue to build on your existing relationship. However, younger age groups will need more sensitive handling. Fortunately divorce is no longer a social stigma, so your child will not be going to school having to face the sometimes cruel taunts of the other kids.

The most difficult age group is the five to 12, where the kids will have a limited understanding of what is going on. It is easier to explain with under fives as they are much more adaptable at that age. Obviously, the nature of your leaving can have a dramatic impact on the communication, depending on whether it was a mutual decision, or whether it was your own or your partner's.

You might not get the chance to tell them yourselves as your ex-partner may have done it for you, especially if it has come to a shock to her as well! Or if she has instigated the divorce, you might find that the job has been done for you. Bear in mind that if your ex-partner has delivered the message then it may have been done with some bias, in which case you may need to give your children a clearer message of what is going on.

TIP

The best possible way to tell your children, especially if they are older than five, is to do it along with your ex-partner.

A joint effort is preferable, as you can agree what you're going to say, and do it together. It can help immeasurably if you and your ex can give as many reassuring messages as possible to your children – just because you are leaving home does not mean that you will never see them again.

If you are unclear about what to say, and how to say it, try to talk to some other divorced dads to find out what they said to their kids, and talk to your friends who have been there before you. Try to deliver your message in a positive light, and, although it might be very difficult, try not to break down and become very emotional. Your kids may be miserable enough without having to know that you are hurting like hell.

Many divorced dads say that this is one of the saddest and most emotional moments in their lives, and that the feelings of letting down their children can be immense. Just as you experienced pure euphoria when your child was first born and you held them in your arms for the first time, this moment can be abject dejection. The only comfort you can take is that it is a credit to your emotional health, and a sign of the strength of your love for your child, that you care so deeply about them. That makes you the dad that you are and will be. This is a moment when you must be brave for your kids; try to do your crying in private later.

Another of the biggest factors in what to tell them will clearly be the circumstances of the separation. If it has been planned mutually and by consent, then you will have other arrangements in place – like where you will be living and so on, which may be information that the kids want to know. If, however, the circumstances were not mutual, then blurting out that your ex is an adulteress and a hussy, or that you have been placed right in the sh** will not help matters.

At this stage, no blame should be attached to either party for the breakdown. Even if you have instigated it, or your partner has, try to take joint responsibility for the breakdown of your relationship. It is not a good start if you are fighting from the off with your ex-partner. At the moment of telling your kids that their world has changed, avoid them seeing and hearing conflict between the two people who are the anchors of their world.

TIP

Little white lies are still lies, and your integrity with your kids is fundamental to your relationship. If they can't trust you, then you will struggle later to develop the relationship you want.

Be careful about telling your children little white lies as a way of softening the blow; it may build up some hope that you should not allow to linger. However timing can be used to great effect. You don't have to tell them everything at once.

◆ Avoid emotional statements and getting over emotional when communicating to your children in the first few weeks.

◆ Think about what to tell them beforehand.

◆ Don't agree to telling a lie because it makes life easier at the time. It will come back to haunt you in the future.

◆ Plan to have plenty of time to talk. Don't do it as they are just going out, or you are on your way to work.

◆ Pick a neutral and public place, especially if you and your ex-partner are in conflict. It could avoid a loud and angry scene.

◆ If the children are teenagers then ensure that you make the conversation a two way process, and get them to open up about their thoughts and feelings.

Finally, having got over the hurdle of telling the children – and for many divorced dads this is a watershed moment which makes everything real – this moment is also the time that will spark a chain of events that lead to a permanent change in both your and your kids' lives. Don't look back to what might have been or what was. That is now in the past and you must look forward to a new life, with new opportunities and new experiences and maybe, in time, new relationships.

DEALING WITH STRESS

Sources of stress

Stress and worry can kill you. Yet it is normal at the time you are going through your separation, and probably for the next six months or so, to have a great deal of anxiety and concerns. You will naturally wonder about the future:

◆ Will you and your children be able to cope?

◆ Will you still be able to see them?

◆ Will you still be a good dad?

Money is probably very short which will cause further stress, let alone wondering what will happen in two years time if your circumstances change. Your relationships with other members of your family could be strained. Stress can be found in a hundred different areas of your life. It all adds up to a potentially deadly time.

There are two major sources of stress. Firstly there is the stress of dealing with the actual problems that you have in your life, and secondly there is stress from perceived or potential problems that you may face. Many divorced dads go through a period where they spend time imagining the worst possible scenarios; haunting images of despair grow in the middle of the night as you lay there mulling over the worst that can happen. These ideas need to be banished from your mind. As always, you need to remember that your relationship with your children is for you to determine.

Let's not beat around the bush. The biggest source of stress and pressure in your life is the one that you place upon yourself. You

Unfortunately, carrying out any kind of retribution, even a mild form of criminal damage, will create more problems than it is worth, even if you get yourself the cast-iron alibi that you were fishing that night with your best mate. You might be able to fool the police, but you won't fool your ex, and she is likely to be less co-operative over your contact with the children. She herself may just decide to go ahead with some of the retribution that she has been planning – and you could end up the worse for it!

Your best course of action is to leave the past behind you. Whatever wrongs have been done to you, you should move on with your life. Of course the motivation to exact some form of revenge on an ex-partner who has wronged you is very strong. But certainly if there are kids involved then any form of retribution will probably have a knock-on effect on the kids. If you damage her car, for example, the cost of repair will mean money not spent on the kids.

2

Seeing your kids:
the first few months

WHAT HELP DO I NEED?

Involving family and friends

You need to look very close to home for help at this time, as the 'State' does not provide any financial or practical support. The only place you can look to is your family and friends; as a result, many divorced dads don't get any help at all with their contact, because they don't live close to their family, or do not have a network of friends that they can lean on. They *do* cope.

TIP
It can be a lot easier, especially in the first few months, if you have somebody to lean on.

Practical support can be something simple like having somewhere to take the kids on a rainy day, (especially if you can't, or your ex won't let you, take the children back to where you are living at the time) to helping out with the transport arrangements if you don't own your own set of wheels.

It can be very useful to have a third person to act as an intermediary between you and your ex-partner if necessary. But be

- Remember that you are one of a thousand divorced dads who are in the same boat. Whilst it is personal for you, you are not being singled out.

- If you know in advance that you will be denied access on a special day, plan to enjoy the day yourself. Do something that is special for you.

CASE STUDY

Access on special days
Dad: Steve
Child: Lauren (aged four when got divorced)

When I separated from my wife, we completed the statement of arrangements for my daughter (under a normal divorce proceeding) and completed a contact order, which detailed the times when I would see my four-year-old daughter.

I had a great solicitor who asked me what I wanted, and made sure that he covered all those times. So when I applied for my contact order I asked for, and got, contact for Easter holidays, summer holidays and some time on other special days like Lauren's birthday. He also put into the contact order some time at Christmas – four days over Christmas on alternate years.

My ex-wife had wanted split access on Christmas day, with me picking up my daughter around 3pm, but I was very uncomfortable about that. Firstly because I would never get to see my daughter open up her presents on Christmas morning and so would never have the chance of being Father Christmas on the actual day. Also, my ex-wife's new partner was very aggressive towards me, and I didn't want to spend any part of my Christmas day in his presence (nor my ex-wife's for that matter).

So although my ex-wife hated the court order, she had to obey. Having those four days gave me the opportunity to do something really special with the time. When Lauren was six, I took her to Lapland, flying out on 23rd and back on 27th December. What a great holiday it was! The tour operator was brilliant, and the whole holiday was as magical as my dreams, and totally enthralling for my daughter.

I was the only single dad in the hotel. I didn't notice this, but after several days some of the other parents asked me where Lauren's mum was – had she passed away? They were all shocked when I told them that I had access for Christmas. In fact, the looks on their faces were a sight in itself. Those four wondrous days were probably the best holiday that I have ever been on and if I had not asked for it in the court order, Lauren and I would not have been able to create some absolutely magical memories together.

HOLIDAYS WITH YOUR CHILDREN

In essence, your children can go on anything that you and your ex-partner can agree. Just like special days, if she is being difficult, follow the same advice: don't try and deal with it immediately. If she's not co-operating; wait and tackle it later.

TIP
If you do get to take the kids away during the first few months, it is important to be as natural with them as possible. It is *not* important that you take them on a trip to some exotic resort or spend lots of money on them.

Going to a meeting is excellent therapy if you are having a nightmare of a time, then you will find people who not only understand your plight but also can offer you some practical advice and support. Sometimes it is just enough to know that you are not the only one who is in the seemingly sinking boat. You might find that the stories you hear make you realise that in fact your position is actually not as bad as some. Attending a meeting and hearing others talk about much more complicated problems than yours can make you feel much better about your own daily dramas, and can put them in perspective.

LOOKING TO THE FUTURE

At some point, the initial period of unrest and change will be over. It is time to now set about becoming the great dad that you always knew you wanted to be, and to build a relationship where you can inspire and have a lot of fun with your children. The first few months are the most emotional and in many ways the hardest time that you will have, but developing a simple parenting plan, which can be built on for later, is a great start. You will encounter problems, you will have some heartache and you will have to compromise a lot. But you can pull through and prosper.

You will get through it. Time stops for no man nor his children, and the natural course of your separation and divorce will take its course, just like thousands of dads around you going through the same process every day.

3

Contact arrangements

When you and your partner split up, the decision that was made was to separate from each other. It is probable that neither of you knew very much about the rights and issues regarding access to your children before you split. It is also probable that neither of you talked to a solicitor about access before making the decision to split. Certainly, most people are too wrapped up in their own lives, which are undergoing massive upheaval, to think that access to the kids will be a problem.

Most couples who break up do so never intending to stop the other party from having unencumbered access to the children. However it is rare that this remains the case – and so inevitably, disputes between the parents over access rights cause a breakdown in the relationship between them. The children themselves are often placed firmly and squarely in the middle of the dispute. This conflict can lead to problems with access to the kids.

There is very little data available about this, but up to 40 per cent of women admitted to having frustrated the access of the father with the child. It is likely that if 40 per cent have actually admitted to it, then the real figure is significantly higher.

In the worst case scenarios, 'parent alienation' occurs where, for a whole host of reasons, the resident parent (normally the mother) sets out to remove the divorced dad from the child's life.

◆ Give them a good brief about your ex-partner and ask them what other cases they have handled that are similar – and what the outcome was in terms of time and cost.

Court order

You need to apply for a court order for the following:

◆ residency
◆ contact arrangements
◆ financial order
◆ prohibited steps (specific issues).

There are two methods that you can choose from.

1 You can get your solicitor to do all the work. They have done many hundreds of these before, and will ensure that all the legal points are covered and that the application is processed in an appropriate manner. They will then ensure that they are available to represent you in court on the day that the request comes in front of the judge.

2 You can do it yourself without the aid of a solicitor. It is actually a simple procedure and starts by filling in a form at the office of the local family court. The staff at the office will be most helpful, if you explain to them what you are trying to do. They will point out which form to complete, and even tell you which boxes are needed and what to do with the completed application form.

It is not a free service; you will have to pay for each court application. The fees depend on the application and are set charges. Expect to pay between £60–100 for an application.

You can, as part of your application, ask for the costs to be considered by the judge, if it is a financial matter. But it is unusual for judges to consider applications for costs on contact issues. In truth in the vast majority of cases, both parties have to incur their own costs.

Divorced dads who are capable and who have been through the process once already generally dispose of the services of a solicitor and act for themselves. This helps to control the costs, and having seen first hand what happens in a court, they feel quite able to represent themselves on most matters.

Court order facts

In 2003, over 67,000 court orders were issued in the UK. Statistics from the family court reveal that this has significantly increased over the last 10 years, from just over 25,000 orders in 1992 to over 67,000 in 2003. The statistics also show that the vast majority of applications for an order end up with one being obtained. But they fail to show the time it takes to get an order, or to represent the torturous process that fathers go through to obtain that order.

As soon as you decide that you need to involve the court system to get improved access to your children you will be thrown into an unfamiliar world which has its own language and rules. You need to learn to understand these very quickly, or it will cost you a great deal in time and money – especially money. There are many divorced dads who have spent thousands of pounds

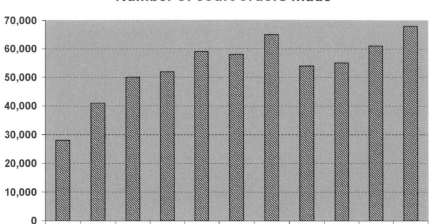

Number of court orders made

attempting to improve contact with their children when much of that cash could have been saved.

Involving the courts can have different effects on your ex. She will react in one of several ways. She may:

◆ understand and agree the need for an independent arbiter in your dispute, and respect the decisions of the court;

◆ become more entrenched in her position;

◆ learn to use the instruments of the legal system against you in your fight for better contact.

At the outset, you need to think very carefully about what action you take and how best to meet your needs and the needs of your children. But most of all you will need to understand some of the processes and UK laws which will determine the outcome of your contact dispute.

You need to understand the following areas. There is a brief explanation of each here; they are covered in more depth later.

- Family court
- Children's Act 1989
- Residency order
- Contact order
- Prohibited steps order
- CAFCASS

Family courts

Your application for contact will firstly be dealt with at a court hearing in the family court. These are in every main town, and all legal matters relating to the Children's Act 1989 and divorce are dealt with there first. These courts sit normally in the same buildings as a county court or magistrates' court, and are only distinguishable by the subject matter. Only if the dispute between the parents cannot be solved in the family court, will the matter be referred to the county or higher court.

Generally, all the normal legal machinations can be used in a family court. Solicitors, barristers, judges, court ushers and officers, and along with these all the costs that are associated with these people.

Children's Act 1989

This is the current piece of legislation that determines the rights of all members of the family in disputes. It was designed to put the interests of the child first, and allow both parents to take an active role in the development of the child. It was drawn up with the intention that parents should seek agreement wherever possible over issues relating to the child. It also takes into account the child's wishes/thoughts and, depending on the age of the child, seeks to consult them and keep them informed of the legal process and be responsive to their needs.

From a divorced dad's point of view there are many problems with the Children's Act. The reasons for this are discussed later in this chapter.

It is worth detailing at this stage that under section 1(3) of the Children's Act 1989, the court must have regard in particular to the following:

◆ The ascertainable wishes and feelings of the child/children concerned (considered in the light of their age and understanding).

◆ The child's physical, emotional and educational needs.

◆ The likely effect of any change in the child's circumstances.

◆ The age/sex/background and characteristics that the court feels relevant.

◆ Any harm which the child has suffered, or is at risk of suffering.

◆ How capable each of the parents, or any other person the court feels is relevant to the child, are.

◆ The range of powers available to the court.

Residency order

Generally, under the terms of a divorce (or if the parents are not married, as a result of a dispute), a residency order will be made, which will set out the living arrangements for the children. In the overwhelming number of cases in the UK, a residency order will be made out in favour of the mother, with some form of contact order made out in relation to the dad.

A further implication to having a residency order is that it is supposed to avoid the removal of the children from the UK, without the written consent of both parents, for periods greater than one month. It also stops the holder of the order from changing the surname of the child.

Contact order

A contact order is designed to protect the rights of a divorced dad to see his children. It is a legally enforceable court order, which determines the nature of the times and dates that the divorced dad can have access to his children. The order would be typically drawn up to cover the following:

- days of contact;

- time and duration of contact;

- arrangements around the collection and drop off of the child;

- telephone access;

- access on special dates e.g. birthdays, Christmas, and other dates;

- sleepover periods.

If the contact is defined in detail, then the order can also be known as a defined contact order. A contact order can be drawn up for any child under the age of 16, and can be varied at any point by either parent, if they feel the order does not provide for the best interests of the child. It is breaches by parents in the provisions of a defined contact order that can be a massive area of conflict between the parents.

Prohibited steps order

A prohibited steps order (sometimes referred to as a specific issues order) can be drawn up by the courts to protect the interests of a child. It is not used for trivial matters, but for major issues – for example if the mother is trying to move abroad, or move schools. If you ever need to take out a prohibited steps order, then you should always involve a solicitor in the application, as generally things need to be done quickly, and they will know if they are any avenues open to you to expedite the legal process.

CAFCASS

CAFCASS stands for Children And Family Court Advisory and Support Service. It is a body of people whose function in court is to assist the judges in making court orders. It is an increasing trend that when a parent applies for a court order (typically because of a dispute over contact or residency), a judge will ask for an independent assessment of the position, and a CAFCASS report to be made.

When there is no dispute, the judge will not ask for a CAFCASS report. In that situation, you will probably not be in a court room, as you and your ex-partner will have made an out-of-court agreement anyway.

The reality is that if a CAFCASS officer has been appointed to your case then inadvertently you are going to be subjected to a lengthy and protracted investigation by what is the court version of the social services. Due to the increasing trend of judges to ask for such a report, it is likely that a CAFCASS officer will not start to look at your case for up to 14 weeks, and is likely to take up to five weeks to complete the process.

The impact that CAFCASS officers will have on your case is significant, and the effect on your access to your child. You will need to understand clearly how CAFCASS can affect your rights – and the key role that this organisation will have on the outcome of your contact dispute.

CAFCASS officers at court

When you and your ex-partner turn up at court on the day of your hearing, it is likely that a CAFCASS officer will talk to you both in an attempt to seek an agreement, prior to either party entering the court room. This service is supposed to be helpful, and avoid lengthy court time and any subsequent reports.

The aim of the CAFCASS officer is to seek a compromise solution to the dispute, and present the judge with an agreement from both parties. This service is free of charge, and can be very useful depending on the skill of the officer.

The problem with this situation is that most CAFCASS officers are looking to reach a compromise between both parents, and it may be that your dispute is not one in which a middle ground is possible. In this case the CAFCASS officer will report to the judge that no agreement has been made. It is likely that if you and your ex-partner wanted to compromise then you would not be at the door of the courtroom in the first place, asking the judge to make a decision. Hence, if you and your ex are in dispute it will be difficult for any CAFCASS officer to reach a compromise position.

Breach of a court order

A breach in a court order happens when one of the parents does not do what the judge has already laid out. This would typically be when child maintenance payments are not made, or access to children does not happen.

As a divorced dad you need to consider if the breach is serious enough to go back to court for enforcement, or to take other steps. The problem you will face is that there is very little that a judge can do to get your ex-partner to adhere to the terms of the order – especially if your case is just starting and is being dealt with in the family court. When you have been through the legal system and progressed to the county court, the judges have more power of enforcement. However, it may take several years and thousands of pounds before you get to that point, especially if your ex-partner is being very awkward and has the resources to pay for a good solicitor.

THE REALITY OF THE CHILDREN'S ACT

It is important to understand why parents go to court for a judge to resolve issues. If parents resort to court they are in dispute about matters concerning their children; these matters will primarily be issues over contact. The purpose of the Children's Act 1989 was to improve the position of all parents and children, but since it has been in force it has failed to do this.

This is because the act was drawn up on the basis that parents are equal, and that therefore each parent would treat the other in an equal manner. But in fact the act has created two classes of parent: the resident and the non-resident parent, and has assigned a set of rights to each.

The act has therefore removed equality between parents and created a sub-class of parent – the non-resident parent (the father in over 90 per cent of cases). The intention of the act was to enable parents to seek agreement, but it has failed to understand the basic fact that if most parents could agree they would do so outside of a courtroom, and that those seeking judicial remedy do so because of a conflict of opinion. As a result, conflict is at the root of all cases which come to the family court.

Here is the area which most divorced dads find is a fundamental flaw in the act. It was drawn up in the belief that parents should be encouraged to seek agreement wherever possible without re-course to the law. This is a marvellous ideal, but given the nature of most split ups and divorces, this is not a concept that is applicable in the real world – especially when you consider that divorces involving children are significantly more complicated than those without.

In fact, the fundamental basis of the act (encouraging parents to seek agreement) is dependent on both parties communicating with each other – and respecting each other's position. Unfortu-nately, this does not happen in the real world, and many divorced dads have to go to court when communication has broken down, and mum has refused to negotiate a solution in an amicable way and maintain an informal agreement.

Areas of contention

The principal area of contention for divorced dads in the Children's Act is that it created the concept of resident parent and contact parent. This has created two classes of parents, with the resident parent having almost total control over the affairs of the children, and the contact parent relegated to a role of visitor in the child's life.

Another area of contention is that the act has no teeth. Let's take the situation where your ex decides unreasonably that she does not want to let you see the kids, and makes up a spurious reason for stopping your contact. Even if you go back to court and the judge sees through her actions and reinforces the court order, the judge is in an almost impossible position to stop her doing it again. This is because their powers of enforcement are few.

Unlike the powers to force you to pay your child maintenance which are many and varied, or the Child Support Agency's powers to enforce its decisions, the family court judge has only two things that he can do: give your ex-partner a slap on the wrist or send her to jail. No judge has yet sent a mother to jail for abusing a court order, as it would be seen to have a detrimental effect on the child for whom she is the resident parent. And as any divorced dad who has to go through this ordeal will discover, a 'telling off' by the judge does not necessarily cut it. In fact all too frequently the mum will re-offend. Sometimes, having learnt that she can get away with it, your ex will continue to abuse access.

The reality of the Children's Act 1989 is clear: don't expect justice and equal rights for most divorced dads.

Court orders and the Children's Act

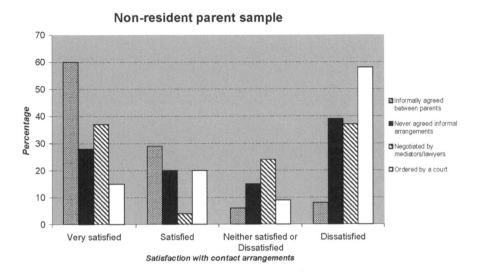

Non-resident parent sample

The recent DfCA study gives very clear evidence as to the level of dissatisfaction for divorced dads when matters are ordered by the court. Over 50 per cent of non-resident parents (typically divorced dads) are dissatisfied with the outcome that a court provides.

The study found that:

On the whole, responding parents who had informally agreed the contact arrangements between themselves were mainly satisfied. These parents were less likely to be dissatisfied than parents of children who agreed the contact arrangements by other methods (82 per cent of parent responses in the resident parent sample and 87 per cent of parent responses in the non-resident parent sample were either satisfied or very satisfied with the contact arrangements).

Satisfaction with contact arrangements that had been ordered by a court or negotiated by mediators or lawyers was low, especially amongst parents from the non-resident parent sample. Over half (57 per cent) of the parents of children whose non-resident parent was the respondent and 26 per cent of parents of children whose resident parent responded to the survey and had their contact arrangements ordered by court were dissatisfied with the contact arrangements.

Over a third (38 per cent) of parent responses for children whose non-resident parent responded and had their contact arrangements negotiated by mediators or lawyers were dissatisfied with the contact arrangements compared with a quarter (26 per cent) of parents of children whose resident parent responded to the survey and had their contact arrangements.

There is clearly a huge contrast between those parents who are in broad agreement, and make informal arrangements (more than 80 per cent satisfaction) and those who have to go through the courts (less than 50 per cent). This is a travesty of justice, but these are the facts.

The fact is, if you are one of the thousands of divorced dads who goes to court to obtain a satisfactory outcome to your dispute, then you have a one in two probability of ending the process very dissatisfied with the outcome, at a cost to you of thousands of pounds and many months' hard work.

CONTACT PARENT

Married fathers

Unless you are in the small percentage of divorced dads who have residency of the children, you lose equal status as a parent, and have to face the reality of being a contact parent. If you were married, a statement of arrangements is generated by your solicitor as part of your divorce.

Most divorced dads who complete a statement of arrangements do so agreeing to the children living with their mother, and in that arrangement a series of contact arrangements with the kids is set out. When a couple split this is often a verbal agreement in the first place, which is then turned into a written statement.

Even though this was the most sensible thing to do at the time, and didn't involve too much disruption for your children, it means that you lose many rights over the ongoing parenting of your children. The only way for a married father to avoid this is to detail in the statement of arrangements that there is shared residency status for the kids.

Unmarried fathers

If you were not married, the situation is much more precarious. Just because your name is on the birth certificate does not mean that you will automatically have parental responsibility for your kids. In fact you may have no legal rights at all, and your ex may make your life very difficult in the future. At the point of separation, if you are unmarried, you should make a legally binding parental responsibility agreement with the mum, which will eliminate a lot of potential trouble in the future. Try and include a statement about shared residency if she will agree, if you want to avoid becoming a contact dad.

As it is the overwhelming case that the mother keeps the family home and residency of the children, then it is the father who has the role of contact parent. In many cases, at the time of separation, the dad has not made adequate arrangements for the provision for the residency of his children at his new home. He probably has not organised things as the financial settlement from the separation has not been completed. Hence the children stay in the family home and the mother automatically gains residency. There is nothing wrong with this, if the mum does not abuse her position and thwart access to the children, but if she does it creates an unequal position from which the dad is likely never to recover.

The reality of the Children's Act 1989 is that there are two classes of parent. The resident parent (normally the mum) and the non-resident parent (normally the dad). This is true unless you do one of two things. Either

◆ obtain shared residency;

◆ don't go to court . . . and obtain agreement with your ex-partner.

Another choice would be to stop all contact with your children. But that is not an option that is recommended, unless in exceptional circumstances (see later in this chapter for more information).

Right from the start of the separation, you have to ask permission from your ex to have access to your kids (unless the children are old enough to make their own arrangements). This was never the original intention of the Children's Act – to allow sole resident parents to control and possibly abuse their dominant position. In fact Section 11 (4) was included in the act to allow shared residency. The legal debate rages on, and if part of section 8 of the act had been written slightly differently, then most of today's problems for divorced dads would be removed.

However, this is of no concern to you if you are subjected to the injustice of becoming a contact parent under the current law. And until the law changes, or judges are given the powers to reinforce court orders, then divorced dads need to understand how to get the best out of the system that they are locked into.

What being a contact dad really means

For most divorced dads, being the contact parent means a continuous struggle to play an active part in the development of their child, and for many it means that their role as dad is sidelined to a bit part which is played only at the times that they are allowed to be with their kids. Most of the dad's views on how the children should be brought up can be ignored, not just by his ex but also by institutions (such as the courts and CAFCASS) – the very organisations which should be there to protect his role in his child's life. Certainly, until the children are young adults and can decide for themselves what course of action they wish to take, then the role of a contact dad has severe limitations on his ability to influence many parts of his child's life.

It is these limitations which cause the greatest frustration. There are limits on the dad's input into:

time spent with the children;

◆ information from schools;

◆ choices for the children;

◆ medical decisions about the children;

◆ where the children live;

◆ how much TV they are allowed to watch;

◆ what their diet is;

◆ what activities they take part in;

◆ who their friends are.

As a contact dad you have limits placed on you. Do not get depressed about it. Turn your energy into spending what time you have with the kids into special time.

◆ Don't get too frustrated.

◆ Don't blame yourself. You are a victim of a legal process that is biased towards the resident parent.

◆ Try to work together with your ex-partner on key issues that you agree on. Then you can tackle the more difficult issues later.

◆ Make the most of the time and experience that you have with your kids: value the day.

◆ Don't worry too much about how the children will grow up; the likelihood is that they will be fine.

◆ Find ways to be involved in their activities (for example, help out at scouts).

◆ Realise the situation that you are in early . . . and come to terms with it. Find ways to improve access and the time that you spend with your children.

◆ Be passive. Don't, under any circumstances, show any form of aggression or abuse towards your ex or the kids.

Asking permission to see your kids

Many divorced dads complain that they now have to ask permission to see their own children. If you are subject to a court order for access, then apart from the defined times that are laid out in the order, or agreed by your ex-partner, you will need to seek the resident parent's agreement (the mum's) to spend additional time with the kids.

Clearly this does not apply if your children are old enough to make their own minds up, and they ring you themselves and make arrangements. But for children still in their formative years, then just turning up at school or where they live is not always a good idea. In fact it can be a bad idea if access is then denied you, because if the children see you but cannot spend any time with you it can create additional stress in their lives. This is something that all responsible dads will want to avoid. You need to get the agreement of the resident parent to have additional time.

Again, the reality of being a contact dad is that additional time is not always forthcoming. A major concern for divorced dads is that the resident parent can abuse their position and control or limit the time that the dad has with the kids. Excuses that they are 'tired after school', 'have homework', or are 'going round to auntie's for their tea', will all stop you having more time with them.

As soon as your children are capable of communicating independently (such as via email or a mobile) then you can talk directly to them and get your ex-partner out of the communication loop. That way you can remove the biggest barrier and avoid having to seek your ex's permission. However, up until that age, the reality of being a contact dad is that you may have to negotiate any extra time with the resident parent, which forces you to communicate with the person that you had to take to court to give you any access in the first place. This is not fair, and is not what the Children's Act intended, but it is the sad reality of life for many contact dads.

Schools

Many divorced dads find that it is not just their ex-partners who freeze them out of their children's lives; many institutions also take the attitude that, as a contact parent, you are now not involved in the upbringing of your kids. Schools can be a major problem area for many divorced dads, a problem that needs to be overcome. Most communication from schools (such as newsletters and so on) is given straight to the children, and goes directly home. So many divorced dads find that they don't know about activities that are taking place, or about other issues relating to their kids.

The Department of Education, however, clearly states:

The parent with whom a pupil does not normally reside is, in the absence of any restriction imposed by the courts, entitled to exercise all the rights which the Education Acts confer on a parent of a child in relation to his or her child, and such a parent should be treated on equal footing with the parent with whom the child lives.

It is unrealistic for you to expect the school to know about a change in your circumstances, when you and your partner separate and you don't live with the children. So you have to contact the school direct to let them know your new address. It is likely that your ex-partner will let the class teacher know about your separation, just in case there are any behavioural issues with your child, so you will probably be spared having to break the news to the school.

But, having contacted the school, don't expect to receive communication without having to chase things up. Many divorced dads are simply ignored. If you find that you are not getting the co-operation that you deserve, then your course of action is as follows:

1) Write to the head of the school.

If that does not work then:
2) Make a formal written complaint to the chair of governors of the school.

If that does not work then:
3) Make a formal complaint to the local authority.

You are entirely within your rights to receive school reports, newsletters, invitations to school events and all other communications . . . so insist upon it.

♦ Contact the head teacher and let him/her know what you want.

♦ Take an active interest in your child's education by attending parents' evenings and so on.

- If your school suggests that you have a joint parents' evening with your ex, and this is not something that you are prepared to do, then explain that.

- If your children are at primary school, make sure that your name appears on any paperwork with regards to parental responsibility, and that you are informed of any issues at school. Most primary schools have a form for each child.

- Don't take being treated as a second-class parent by the teachers.

Your children's health

As a contact parent, there will be many hours where your children will be away from you, and away from your care. So there will be times when you are not around when they have to go to the doctor's or to hospital with their mum. Clearly, no divorced dad would stand in the way of treatment for his kids, and would readily back his ex-partner in actions that protect the health of the children.

However, most of the time that your children become sick, you probably don't get to find out about it, or are not present at the doctor's appointment, so you are only presented with the evidence that your ex-partner gives you. You may not be happy with this, and try to get the information direct from the doctor. Here you may encounter a problem as many doctors will not give you access to your child's medical records, even though you are the dad.

The law in this matter is quite clear. If a child is over the age of 16 then only they have a right to see their medical records. If the child is under 16, then under the Access to Health Records Act 1990, you *don't* have the right to gain access to them.

The Act requires:

Doctors, dentists or other health professionals to provide access to health records in response to a request by the parents . . . or an application can be made by any person with parental responsibility.

However under Section 4 (2) the act states that the patient (effectively the child) needs to consent, or it needs to be in the best interests of the child to consent, for the doctor to agree to the application.

In fact, doctors are the only person who can make a judgement about whether allowing access to records is in 'the best interests' of any child that they have as a patient, and may withhold information from parents as they see fit. This is not a position that has been engineered against divorced dads, but one that actually works for both parents as doctors may withhold information from mothers as well as fathers.

The legal stance here is to protect the confidentiality of the record for the child, even though it feels like a barrier to the divorced dad getting to know what is going on.

The biggest problem: time
The biggest problem faced by divorced dads is that simply they do not spend enough time with their kids. When they lived at the family home they could spend time each day with the children,

but when the father is no longer resident at the same address, contact is limited to those hours laid down either by a court order or by the permission of the ex-partner.

Because of pressures in your life, work, and other commitments, your weekly time with the kids can be down to as little as five or ten per cent of the time that you spent with them at home. Clearly your influence in their lives is therefore lessened. This is the reality of being a contact dad.

It is not a comfortable situation, and it takes several years before many divorced dads realise that their role in their kid's lives is that of a visitor rather than of a traditional dad. It's easy to say, 'spend as much time with the kids as you can', and this of course is the only way to increase the influence that you have with them. But for many that is difficult, as either their ex-partner will not allow it or their own time pressures do not. And time pressures in fathers' lives can change, maybe even starting a second family, and having new responsibilities. It may mean that the available time that can be set aside for children from a previous relationship is squeezed.

Divorced dads who are not in conflict with their ex-partners can still have a problem, as circumstances change, or work or other life pressures take away their time. Even keeping certain hours during the week to spend with the children, many divorced dads feel as if gradually, over time, their impact on their child's life is lessened. This leads to a feeling of helplessness and can be very depressing.

TIP

Try to look on the bright side: many dads who are still living at home feel as if the kids are not taking any notice of them, and the influence that they have on their children is low.

So divorced dads should not despair, as the natural process of growing up is one that will happen whether you are resident at the home or not. Some divorced dads feel that because they are not resident at the family home during the teenage years they are not faced with the hormone releases, mood swings and rebellions, and they can enjoy many benefits of being a dad without having to endure five years of living with the Harry Enfield character Kevin.

They can act as a real friend during those years, without having to get heavy with the kids for all the domestic misdemeanours like never tidying the bedroom, or never helping out around the house. So being a contact dad may in fact be an advantage during the teenage years.

The challenge to all divorced dads is to ensure that during the formative years (three to 11) they create a bond and relationship with their kids that is based on a positive and open relationship, in which the child can trust the dad. If you build trust in this time, and combine it with heaps of love and support, then you will find that you will enjoy the same relationship with your children as many resident dads.

TIP

Always work at creating a positive, loving and trusting relationship with your children, even if you only have minimal contact during their formative years.

CASE STUDY

Changing circumstances

Dad: Dave
Child: Megan
Situation: Married for four years, divorced for five.

My ex-wife and I met through work, when we were both working in Manchester. She was originally come from Gloucestershire, so when we split up, she wanted to return back to her family roots, taking my daughter with her. I understood – she was always close to her family. However my family are all from Manchester, which is where the old family home was, and because of this and work I was not able to relocate to be nearer my daughter. She was three years old when we split up – she is 10 years old now.

My ex-wife and I get along OK. There was never any animosity between us – we accepted that our relationship was not going to work long term, and that Megan was a good thing that had come from it. We have always managed to co-operate with issues over Megan.

I love my daughter, but I don't get to see her very often because she lives so far away. I can't get to see her during the week, or even at weekends, so I have to maintain my relationship with her during the school holidays. I would love it if she lived closer, but I have to deal with the realities of her new life, and that I can only be a part of it for a few weeks of the year.

I have always encouraged her to come up and stay whenever she can and always kept my holiday time at work available for her. At least when she does come up I really get to spend quality time with her. I did consider seeing her at weekends, but the travelling time was over 12 hours and it was just not worth it for the time that was left at a weekend. And I simply could not afford to do the journey regularly.

At first it really bothered me, not knowing a lot about the way in which Megan was growing up. But I trust my ex-wife to do the best for her, so now I am much more relaxed about things. I contribute whatever I can financially, and make sure that I take an interest in her school and other activities. My ex is pretty good and keeps me informed about any important issues, so at least I feel I know what is going on, even if I cannot be a real influence in her daily life.

I sometimes wonder if only seeing Megan for only a few weeks of the year means that she views me as any less of a dad. At the moment, she is too young to make that judgement. Fortunately my ex is very supportive – she understands that she made the move away and that I could not follow – so she never undermines me or tries to belittle the efforts that I do make in Megan's life. I am glad that I continue to do what I can, and see her when I can. I am very proud of the way in which she is growing up.

Contact dad vs stepdad

Possibly the biggest problem in being a contact parent is that you have to make way for other adults to spend time with your kids. It is unrealistic to assume that your ex-partner will shoulder the burden of childcare on her own or that she will not move on in her life. At some point she may well have a partner who will not only interact with the kids, but may also live under the same roof.

While you probably won't have a problem with grandma or auntie taking childcare responsibilities, and having an impact on your child's life, the presence of another man who moves into your ex's life can be a source of stress and anger. This can be exasperated if he then starts spending more time with the children than you do, bringing them up in a different way than you would. It is even worse if it happens in your old family home. Stepdads can be great for your kids, but unless they can respect your position in your children's lives, then problems will occur. Sadly, you cannot tell any stepdad, or new partner of your ex, how you want them to interact with your children. It is simply not an option.

This is a classic scenario faced by many divorced dads, and one you can do nothing about, as you no longer have the right to influence who your ex-partner has in her life. It is a by-product of her new relationship that the new man will spend time with your kids, and have an impact on them (good or bad). (Handling stepdads is an important issue and is covered in more detail later.)

How your child thinks of you

This will depend on the age and awareness of your child. It will depend on how much they understand about your separation, as well as the extent to which they have already established a relationship with you. If you have already created a bond with your kids, then you are better off than a dad who has yet to establish a relationship with his children. Clearly, your children themselves will go through their own personal trauma not having you around the house all the time, and will have to cope with their feelings about the separation of their parents.

If the children are in their teenage years, then the likelihood is that they will come to terms more quickly and easily with the change than you will.

TIP

Remember that your relationship with your children is for you to determine.

If your child is older than about three, their perception of you as a proper dad is already implanted in their mind, whether you were a good attentive dad or spent most of your time at work and in the pub. The key now is to concern yourself with what they think of you as a contact dad. You can create the impression that you wish.

If your children are younger than about three then you may not have spent enough time bonding with the child for them to realise that you are their father, and your job will be much more difficult. Once again, you have to focus on the present, not the past and try not to allow your feelings about not being there for them affect the image that you portray to them. You need to be positive about the contact time that you have, so that they feel as if it is something that you really value.

Be positive about your role as contact dad.

- Never have conversations like, 'If I saw you more we could do XYZ'. Make sure that in the time that you do see them they do XYZ.

- Never tell them that you feel helpless, or depressed, because they will feel responsible for your sadness.

- Always tell them that you are looking forward to seeing them again.

- Always tell them how much spending time with them means to you.

- Never complain to them about subjects that they don't control, such as their time. Wait until they are older and can change it for themselves.

Your child's perception of you as a contact dad depends very much on how you interact with the child. It is now totally in your hands to get on with it. The one thing that can never be changed is that as the real dad, your genes and DNA are ever present in your child's make up, which means that a special bond will always exist between you.

This bond will be tested over time, and that certainly happens when the time that you have with the child is limited. But the bond can never be severed, even if you lose contact. Your role as a dad is to try to nurture that bond whenever you can, given the circumstances that you face, even when your role is as one of contact dad.

MANAGING CONTACT

Conflict at drop offs and collections

Being a contact dad often means that you have to go and pick up your children from your ex-partner's residence, and often you are responsible for dropping them off as well. The reality of being a contact dad is that you won't get equality in this aspect either, especially if your ex-partner now lives away from you. Your ex may well have the attitude that if you want to see the children, then it is up to you to come and pick them up; why should she make life easy for you?

It is not fair that you have to go to the time and expense of travelling to the place where the kids live, but then life is not fair. For most divorced dads extra travelling is a burden that they just have to face.

If you have a court order for access, then amongst the issues you can specify arrangements for collections and drop offs, and try and base the arrangements on a shared basis. The problem you will get, as we have already seen with court orders, is that if your ex-partner decides not to comply, then your only course of action is to drive over and pick up the kids.

The biggest problem that occurs at collections and drop offs is that it is the time when you are most likely to come into contact with your ex-partner. For many divorced dads it is the time when tempers fray and incidents can occur. In fact, collection and drop offs can turn out to become a very stressful experience for both parents, but more so for the kids, who frequently witness acts of aggression or violence between the two people that they love the most. For many children of divorced parents, the danger at is that they have a memory of conflict and violence, which clearly needs to be avoided.

Avoid conflict at collection and drop-off times. Beware: if you lose your temper at a collection or drop off, then you may have to face the consequences. These can be severe. For example:

◆ You may be subject to a police investigation, with your ex-partner accusing you of assault or affray. This will lead to a criminal record.

◆ Your ex-partner may, via her solicitor, refuse to give you access to your children as a result of the alleged behaviour.

◆ Your ex-partner may well return to court for a change in the defined court order for access and reduce your contact with your kids.

The one thing that you can be guaranteed is that any allegation made about you will be exaggerated and cause you a lot of stress. You don't need to add to the stress and anger that you are already feeling when you have to face the ex.

The most important thing to think about at this point in time is the children. They have probably been looking forward to spending the day with you all week, so don't allow their time with you to start off on a downer. You want them to be looking forward to your contact time in a positive light, not dreading the moment that mummy and daddy have a row at the front of the house, when mummy is in tears, and daddy in an angry mood for the rest of the day.

You need to avoid putting this conflict and stress in their lives. This is part of the responsibility that you have as the adult; find a different way to vent your anger and emotions, not on the object of them (your ex) to the detriment of those that are simply the innocent victims of the divorce – your kids.

Giving the children back

Many divorced dads say that when the time for contact comes to an end, and they have to take the kids back to their home, it can be a very depressing moment.

It is a reminder of the fact that the dad is returning to his life, and that the children are not a big part of it. So you will not be the only divorced dad who feels this; it is perfectly natural and is an emotion that unfortunately you will just have to come to terms with.

You need to develop strategies for coping with it. What you don't want to do is to project your sadness onto the kids; it will make them feel responsible and is quite unfair. You need to tell them how much you are looking forward to the next contact and let them know about any plans that you have for that time. It is great if they are a little older to ask them what they want to do, and get their input. It may be that your kids are feeling a little sad as well, with the thoughts of not seeing you for a while. The positive thing to do here is to give them something to look forward to, rather than sending them home depressed as well.

If you don't feel great after you have given the kids back to their mum, then you also need to look after yourself a bit. Try to spend the time immediately afterwards with friends or family, and not be on your own, brooding about what contact you don't have. Or spend the time planning your next contact. Whatever you choose to do, the reality of being a contact dad is one of constantly giving back your kids and spending time without them.

SHARED RESIDENCY: THE PROPER ARRANGEMENT

There is only one way which will enable the divorced dad to minimise negotiations with his ex with regard to access, and that is to ensure that when they split up she agrees to him having shared residency status for the children.

When you split up, ensure that your ex-partner agrees as part of the divorce discussions for you to have shared residency rights over your children. This is probably the important rule in this book, so ensure that you read the following pages carefully.

TIP

Shared residency can dramatically improve your access throughout your child's life.

What is shared residency?

It means that you have an equal right to decisions about your child, such as schooling, activities, and health. It also protects your rights to have access to your children. In practice, it does not necessarily mean that your child lives with you for 50 per cent of the time. This may not be desirable, either from your perspective or that of your child.

In fact the law says it

. . . should be flexible enough to accommodate a much wider range of situations. In some cases, the child may live with both parents,

even though they do not share the same household. It was never our intention that children should share their time more or less equally between the parents. Such arrangements will rarely be practicable, let alone for the child's benefit.

Law Commission 1998 report on the
wording of Section 11(4) of the Children's Act 1989.

By achieving shared residency you can avoid many of the issues that as a contact parent make you a second-class parent. You will be treated in the courts as an equal parent, not one who is only a bit part in your child's life.

When to get shared residency

When you were still together and living at the family home you automatically had shared parental responsibility with your partner. It was on that basis that you had a family in the first place. You need to use all your powers of persuasion with your ex-partner to draw up the terms of your divorce with shared residency as the basis of your relationship with your children.

If the situation is that as a dad you and your ex-partner were never living in the same house, then clearly, the situation is different, and it will be a lot more difficult to get your ex to agree to shared residency. You may even have a struggle to get your name on the birth certificate.

At the start of your separation, get your partner to agree to a shared residency order for the children.

◆ You don't need to explain the full implications of shared residency.

- Persuade your ex with phrases such as, 'We are both the parents – I want the kids to know that we share the responsibility.'

- Don't use bribes – use negotiation.

- Raise the subject of shared residency when you start to talk about separation.

- Make sure that your ex-partner knows that you are not trying to take the kids away from her home, and that shared residency does not have to mean that the kids live with you 50 per cent of the time.

- If you have already separated try to introduce the subject, but not via your solicitor, as she will immediately get her solicitor to give her advice which will probably be not to consider it.

- Don't make an application to the court without talking to her first – it will just be a waste of time and money. If you do apply to the court you will need her support unless you want a real fight.

Sole residency

When a couple get divorced, their children continue to live with their mother, and under the terms of the divorce settlement a statement of the child's arrangements are made by the court.

In the overwhelming majority of divorces, the residency of the child is given to one parent (normally the mother) and a contact order may also be made, detailing the allowed contact with the other parent. In fact, sole residency gives the resident parent a power over access that was never intended under the Children's

Act 1989, and remains the biggest obstacle to a divorced dad in maintaining an unencumbered relationship with his children.

Most divorced dads do not realise the significance of this when they agree to it, thinking that it is normal. By agreeing to mum becoming the resident parent and themselves the contact parent, they subjugate their position in legal terms for the rest of the child's life.

This is the first surprise that most divorced dads get when they start to look into how to get more access to their kids, or how to get protection from the courts with issues over access. They discover that as a contact, not a resident parent, they are in fact a second-class parent.

CASE STUDY

Residency of the children
Dad: Ron
Children: One boy and one girl (aged eight and six when separated)
Situation: Married for 21 years, separated for nine years

My ex-wife simply announced one day that she was fed up, and left the marital home. As it turned out later she was seeing another man, who she went to live with. At the time the kids were six and eight years old.

I asked her if she wanted to take the kids with her, as initially I felt that they would be better off with her. To my surprise she did not seem to want that, so I had to think if I wanted residency of the children. So I asked her again but she was adamant that she wanted a different life (maybe the fact that she was going to live with another man had something to do with it), so I started to think about having the children live with me.

The kids themselves had no preconceptions – they were too young to decide or to know what was best for them. Through my solicitor I drew up a statement of arrangements for the divorce that gave me sole residency and detailed contact times for my ex-wife. This was definitely the best option. It meant stability for the children as I continued to live in the family home, and my ex was distracted by her new relationship. Financially it was hard as she got 50 per cent of the family home, so I had to re-mortgage to stay living there. What made it really tough was that her contribution via the CSA was pretty minimal.

At first my family were surprised but supportive. Even to this day they have not forgotten or forgiven my ex for walking out.

Since the early days I have had very little communication with my ex. I don't even know how she feels about the kids. I don't really care; I never talk to her these days. The kids still see her now and again, and have a week's holiday with her in the summer.

So for the last nine years I have had the children live with me on my own. I have never regretted this even through it has been really hard work. Being a single dad is tough – balancing, work, childcare and money as well as trying to have a bit of a life of your own, but somehow I have managed. Having the kids and seeing them grow up has been the main emphasis in my life.

I am really proud of my achievement. Mark is now 17 years old and growing into a great bloke – he is very helpful and sensitive. Amy is a teenager so I am going through the usual problems that a dad has with a teenage daughter. I have had to do it on my own as their mum has never really been around to be supportive and never got involved with some of the growing up pains. I think that is why the kids don't have much of a relationship with her now and rarely see her. In my experience a man can do just as good a job at bringing up the kids as a woman – providing he gives a lot of love, a lot of attention and a great deal of care.

For the last four years the kids and I have lived on a narrow boat. At first they loved it but now Amy wants her own space, which I can understand, whereas Mark loves it to bits and wants to have his own boat.

Having residency of the kids has not stopped me doing what I wanted; my plan was always to be a great dad and see them through their childhood, which I have done. Now that they have grown up a bit I get some time for myself and can do a little fishing and stuff.

CONTACT ABUSE

Misery, misery, misery . . . is the inevitable consequence of what happens when the mum stops the dad from seeing the kids as per the agreed contact/access times. It is absolute misery for all the parties involved: misery for the child, misery for the dad, and the most miserable part about it is that it happens as much as it does.

A huge number of divorced dads report that at some point their contact with their children has been abused by the resident parent. A visit to a meeting of the Families Need Fathers support group in your local area will provide you with as much evidence as you need to tell you that this problem is widespread and leads to more hostility between parents than any other subject. A visit to a meeting of Fathers4Justice showed how angry divorced dads are about the lack of protection that the law gives them in this area, and how little the current legal set-up recognises this as a real social problem.

Contact abuse comes in two forms. Firstly, when the resident parent stops contact altogether, and secondly when the mum frustrates contact on occasions. Both forms of abuse can be equally frustrating for a divorced dad who seeks to develop and maintain a relationship with his kids.

On the day
Stories of dads turning up on the doorstep of the mother's house to discover that nobody is in, or the door is not answered, are commonplace. Phone calls telling the dad he can't have the children as per the court order are a polite way of breaching the order. Some mothers even get their solicitors to write to the father telling him that he cannot see the kids at such-and-such a time. In the worst cases scenarios the resident parent doesn't allow any form of contact – even though this is contrary to what may have already been set out by a judge in a contact order. Each mum will justify their actions on some grounds and seriously believe that they are acting in the best interests of the kids. Even their solicitors will back them and agree to the breach.

The problem is compounded by the fact that the courts or police will not come to the father's aid and enforce any order for his ex-partner to hand over the kids. Under UK law there is no course of action that can take place on the day if the mum abuses her position and refuses to hand over the children. The police will not come out and help you, treating the matter as a civil rather than criminal breach and therefore not their domain. In fact, the situation is likely to be turned against the father if the police see him as creating a disturbance. If he kicks off at all he may well be arrested for a breach of the peace, or worse.

TIP
Don't let your anger turn to any kind of violence.

Some dads really feel angry – really angry. They allow their emotions to get the better of them, lashing out at property, or worse at their child's mother, as they feel so helpless. This is likely to have several consequences.

Firstly, the ex will see this as justification of her act, and is likely to refuse further access to the kids. Secondly, the children themselves will be negatively affected by such actions, maybe even start to be fearful of their dad and scared for their mum – with whom they feel a natural bond. Thirdly, when you finally get back to court and the CAFCASS officer investigates your case, they may report that you are a violent man who scares the kids, and recommend that your access rights be severely limited again. CAFCASS will see the fact that your ex-partner has breached the court order in the first place as almost irrelevant.

Don't expect justice and equal treatment from the courts, its officers or the police, because you will not get it. If your ex-partner abuses your rights of access and does not allow you contact with the children then, on the day, there is absolutely nothing you can do about it.

If contact is breached by mum on the day, *never* create an incident at the family residence, and *never* give her a reason to go to court and persuade a judge that your contact should be limited, or even stopped.

◆ Write a letter to your ex-partner telling her that you have made a record of the breach and will go to court if contact is not permitted.

◆ Keep a diary of all instances where access has been abused.

◆ If the kids are old enough to have separate communication, ring or email them letting them know that you are available when they wish to see you.

◆ Get rid of your anger by some means other than violent behaviour.

◆ Don't plot twenty ways to kill your ex.

◆ If your ex-partner consistently abuses your contact, learn to understand why and seek to address the real issue.

◆ Ask your ex-partner if she wishes to go to mediation to resolve the issues (do so in writing) rather than avoid a lengthy and costly court process.

◆ If you can have a conversation with your ex-partner, ask her if she is prepared to give you an alternative, and see if you can work around it.

Understanding your ex-partner's real intentions

If your ex-partner is abusing your contact, the first thing that you should do is to stop yourself and ask, why is she not allowing you a fair degree of contact with your child?

You need to understand the reason if you are to work out how to best overcome her real objection and enjoy fewer obstacles to your contact. It is very unlikely that she thinks your contact is harmful to the kids, and that you will kidnap them – or worse. It is more likely that she is reacting to a situation that she does not like, not for any reason that is driven by the needs of the child.

This, however, will not stop her telling the CAFCASS officer any old story to back up her actions, and she will probably come up with some plausible stories. If the child is young she might claim that they are wetting themselves with worry about having to see dad. Or if the child is older, between five and ten, she could make up any number of reasons. The best thing is to recognise her intentions before it becomes a serious problem and goes to court.

Below is a list of reasons that your ex-partner might try to stop you having fair access to your children. It is not an exhaustive list, but they are some of the more common reasons why mums try to get back at dads.

Money
This is top of the list.

Your ex-partner may feel that you are not paying enough for your kids, and that the best way to get you back is to stop you from seeing them. If this is the case then she is not likely to admit it outright, other than to make jibes along the lines of, 'You don't pay for them, so you don't have the right to see them.' She won't think about the fact that, legally, contact with the children is a totally separate issue to child maintenance; actually it is your children that have the right of access to you. If money is the motive for her actions, then your problems are not likely to go away in the short term – unless of course you pay her what she wants.

Many divorced dads pay more than they should, for an easy life and unencumbered access to their children. What is more important in life: a few quid, or your relationship with the children? But you need to decide where your limits are – and then stick to them.

If you do give in, then ensure that you keep a record of all payments and try to avoid cash. If you buy things like school uniform or shoes, then keep the receipts – it may be of use later if you go to court. Also, when the children grow up, you can prove to them that you did more than you needed to help in their upbringing, even if their mum has told them otherwise.

Happy families

Another major reason for your ex-partner to abuse contact is because you have become an inconvenience to her if she has a new man in her life. She may want to create a new happy family at her home – which includes the new man and not you. She may, if your child is very young, seek to replace you with her new man as the child's father.

When there is a new relationship, some women feel that it is their new man who should take the role of dad in the child's life, because it is the new partner who is living at home and not you. It creates a new happy family at home; quite naturally what she wants to create in her home. The fact that you turn up every week and remind her of a failed relationship will only serve to destroy the family that she is now striving to create. The fact that your child is yours – and has a right of access to you – is quite simply not in her thinking.

There is not much you can do in this case. It would be no good to turn around and tell her what she is doing is morally wrong, or not in the best interests of the children, or that it will have long-term implications for the child. It will not matter to her what your opinion is, as she will not value your thoughts on the matter.

Don't try to enter a conversation with her about her motives for the contact abuse; simply keep working at a remedy with her. You could always suggest that you both go to mediation before you take court action. It is probably not advisable to talk to her new man – unless you can avoid being perceived as going behind her back. And he may well have been fed a story about you which is not accurate, and so will not be receptive.

Jealousy

Jealousy is a very powerful and destructive emotion.

There are countless tales of women who act out of jealousy, especially if they think that you have become involved with another woman. Of course she can become jealous of you at any time, whether it is at the time of your separation, or later when you are rebuilding your life with another relationship. If she is jealous and wants to get back at you, your contact abuse may suffer as she uses the most powerful weapon in her armoury to hurt you – your children.

She may be jealous for any number of reasons. You may be benefiting from your new-found freedom, or have lost a few pounds in weight, or started activities that simply make you happy. These things may make your ex-partner envious, especially if she feels that she is still stuck at home, and tied down by parental responsibility – never with a moment to herself.

It may be that your ex-partner comes to terms with her feelings and is only affected by jealousy when on a 'downer'. If the contact abuse doesn't seem to have a pattern and no obvious cause, then it is likely that your ex-partner is acting out of jealousy. The question is, of course, how to address the issue. Confronting her will be of little use as she is probably in denial about her emotions – you will have to have a much more subtle approach.

Revenge

They say that hell hath no fury like a woman scorned (although in fact the real verse, by William Congreve, is 'Heaven has no rage like love to hatred turned/Nor hell a fury like a woman scorned').

Contact abuse at the time of your separation can in many cases be put down to revenge, especially if you were the one to leave the partnership. If your ex-partner feels she has been wronged, she may take revenge by stopping you seeing the kids.

But it is not only at the initial separation that your ex-partner can be driven by revenge. If, for example, your divorce settlement did not go quite the way she wanted it to, you are liable to have another instance of contact abuse at a later date.

Revenge can be the most violent of reactions, but is normally short-lived, manifesting itself in an explosive act of defiance. There are tales of women damaging their ex-partner's cars or possessions, but contact abuse is just as violent a reaction. Your ex may feel she is getting her own back at you, irrespective of what the children want and need.

TIP

The best possible way of dealing with revenge is not to react, as this will let your ex-partner know precisely how to get at you.

It is best to play it down and to step away; let it blow over like the proverbial storm. However, if you are unlucky and it continues, you need to use the old 'reverse psychology'. If you show that you are concerned only with the children and their feelings, and don't let her know how much you are hurting when she abuses contact, she will start to focus on their reactions not yours. Even if you are in a blinding rage because she won't let you see them, it has to seem as if your feelings are irrelevant and you don't really care about the effect her actions are having on you.

This may be very difficult. She may even engineer situations where she can see your reaction firsthand, perhaps for example you get to the door of her house before she tells you that the kids have gone to stay with their grandma. But you must not react. If she sees a chink in your armour she is likely to twist the knife until she feels that you have bled enough. You need to get her to think that her actions are helping you, not hindering you.

It's best to make it seem that, by stopping you seeing the kids, you can get on with other things; far from being a hindrance to your happiness, her actions allow you to seek pleasure elsewhere. If she starts to think that you are benefiting from her actions she will soon stop or change. If, however, your ex really has got it in for you and wants revenge to the extent that you won't even be left with the shirt on your back then you have a different problem. This revenge can result in 'parent alienation syndrome'.

Dealing with contact abuse

Clearly, there is nothing that you can achieve on the day that your contact time is abused and your ex-partner stops you from having access. If the problem becomes ongoing, you need to look for a solution. After you have accepted the fact that you are not going to see the children at the time which was previously agreed, then you need to decide what – if anything – you are going to do about it. Your reaction may well depend on whether you think the problem is a short or long-term situation. You need to stand back and make an assessment of the problem: how big it is, how long it is going to last, and what is going to be the best way to get what you need and want – time with your child.

Dos and Don'ts when contact is stopped

- ◆ **Do** make a record (diary) of events and actions.

- ◆ **Do** work out why your ex-partner is doing it.

- ◆ **Do** write to her and ask for her proposals for access. These may well be unacceptable, but at least you can try.

- ◆ **Do** talk to other divorced dads to see what they have done.

- ◆ **Do** talk to another member of her family (maybe her mum) and see if you can get someone to act as a third party to resolve the problem quickly.

- ◆ **Do** be prepared to eat humble pie – a large slice of it. Your ex-partner may want to use the kids as a tool to get something from you and it may be easier to agree at this stage.

- ◆ **Do** remember that the children's needs are best served when parents remove conflict from the situation – do everything that you can to avoid confrontation.

- **Don't** get angry on the doorstep or on the phone. Remain calm about it (at least in front of your ex-partner – you can vent your anger elsewhere).

- **Don't** try to kidnap the kids.

- **Don't** phone them later and abuse their mum. It will split their loyalty, put them under severe emotional pressure and be stressful for them.

- **Don't** go to the pub and get drunk – it will make you feel more depressed.

- **Don't** underestimate the problem, if your ex-partner is likely to make this a long-term problem, you need to get your act together and try to stop her.

- **Don't** give in.

If your ex-partner is adamant that she will not let you have access to the kids, one possible move is to find out what it is that she wants – if there is something – and give it to her, at least temporarily. You may, for example, need to appease her by giving her some more money. This may buy you a little time to talk directly to your kids and explain to them, if they're old enough, how much you love them and want to see them, but because you and mum are in dispute, mum may stop you. In other words, let the kids know that if you can't see them it is not because you don't want to, but because you are not allowed to.

It is a good idea, if you think that your ex may stop your access at some point in the future, to have that chat with your kids. Because forewarned is forearmed, and if you can persuade them that you are not the problem, then they will at least not be sitting at home wondering if their dad still loves them.

Short-term contact abuse

Short-term contact abuse is one of divorced dads' biggest frustrations. It happens when an arrangement you have to see the children is not kept by your ex-partner. She might cancel on the day, or tell you a few days before that your child has something else to do. Divorced dads need to be flexible as occasional upsets will occur, and should be expected; children do become ill, or get invited to a friend's party at a time when they usually spend time with their dad.

However, abuse occurs when the reason for removing contact is driven by the needs of the mum and not by the needs of the child, or when your wishes about a change in arrangements are not respected.

TIP

Contact times will need to be flexible to cope with events such as parties, birthdays and other activities.

No divorced dad objects to this. It is only when changes are motivated by the needs of the mum – for example when she goes away for the weekend taking the kids with her but doesn't offer alternative arrangements. You have a right to get upset if this happens, to feel angry if no alternative is provided.

Almost all divorced dads have to put up with a degree of short-term contact abuse, and it would be unrealistic for you to expect otherwise. Unfortunately it comes with the territory. The question is, at what point do you take action, and what can you do about it?

It is impossible to say, for example, that X number of changes are reasonable, and any more than this is contact abuse. It is as long as a piece of string – it depends on what you are prepared to tolerate, and how much you believe your ex-partner.

Unfortunately, options for solving the problem are extremely limited, as once again it is the resident parent who holds the power in these circumstances. If you already have a court order for access, then you can return to the court and get a judge to reinforce the order by telling your ex-partner that she has to comply with the terms of that order.

However, the Children's Act – upon which your order for access was drawn up – has no realistic method to enforce her to change her ways. So going to court to solve short-term abuse can be a waste of time and money. In fact it can be detrimental, as it might inflame your ex-partner and also show her that even by going to the courts there is very little you can do to stand in her way. Conversely, of course, she may not appreciate the stress and time and money that is involved – and think twice about doing it again.

But most divorced dads don't have a court order and their only option is to negotiate with their ex-partner and try to convince her that she should act more honourably. The flaw here is that your negotiating position is non-existent as she holds all the cards as the resident parent.

TIP

Short-term contact abuse tends to occur in situations where there is a lack of respect by the resident mum towards the divorced dad, and this of course is not conducive to successful negotiations.

The other option that you have is to do nothing. On that day, and maybe for a few weeks, remember the old saying 'slowly, slowly, catch a monkey'. If you let your ex-partner know that her actions have upset you, then depending on the relationship that you have with her, she might be tempted to continue to abuse your contact.

As mentioned earlier, you may need to use a bit of reverse psychology. If she feels she has hurt you then, as her actions are designed to do just that, she may continue to use the kids to get back at you. However, if her actions did not have the desired effect, and she had to entertain the kids for the day and put up with complaints from them that they wanted to see you, she may decide that stopping you seeing the children has the effect of adding to your freedom and benefits your life. You may find that doing nothing, and showing no reaction, is the best possible option for you.

Again, communication is the key to resolving any dispute. Irrespective of what your immediate reaction to short-term abuse is, somewhere down the track you will need to sort out the problems, and this can only be done if you communicate. If she won't communicate with you then you have very little chance of stopping the short-term abuse, but if you can open a channel of communication – you can at least negotiate, even from the lowly position that you are in.

Communicating with your ex

◆ Adopt a flexible approach from the start; try to negotiate over contact times rather than get to a position where contact is terminated.

◆ Find ways to improve the notice you are given about changes to avoid last-minute changes and the frustration that this leads to.

◆ If your child is old enough to communicate with, seek their input into any changes that need to be made.

◆ Be prepared to lose out sometimes, but remember that any small gains are worthwhile and can be built on.

◆ Remember that this is a long-term situation – a war can be won, even if some battles are lost.

◆ Although you can always go to court and get a better deal, it is not that enforceable. It is better to change the terms from the point where you start your negotiation.

◆ Keep a diary of all instances of contact abuse.

◆ Keep a record of your attempts at communication.

Failure to communicate will only lead to a continued stalemate, and leave the courts as the only option. This should really only be your final option. Short-term abuse is best dealt with in a relaxed and open way, but if your relationship with your ex-partner does not allow this then these problems are likely to persist and you will have a longer-term abuse problem. Short-term abuse will turn into a problem which becomes much more difficult to solve.

Long-term contact abuse

Your response will be different if you think the problem is long term. You will probably have to contact a solicitor and start the legal process rolling; not that this will solve your problem and get you access to your children. In fact by stepping up into a legal gear you may find that your ex-partner is alienated even more, resulting in continued contact abuse. You will need to decide your course of action, but before doing so you need to attempt to solve the problem itself, by understanding and reacting to the true motive.

TIP

It is *always* best to avoid legal action.

If you think you can solve the problem between you and your ex-partner then you should try that first. If you think the contact abuse could be a long-term problem you need to open a channel of communication with your ex-partner. Nothing can be done until you have done that. Of course, this is likely to prove very difficult as she may not wish to talk to you. In fact it may take you several attempts to discuss matters with her, and when you do get to talk, many other influences will be at work too.

Dealing with long-term contact abuse

◆ Start with communication rather than solicitor action. Only if she refuses your attempts at communication should you tell her that if you can't sort it out between you, you will have to take the matter further and instruct a solicitor.

◆ It may not be possible to talk to her directly; if she does not want to, be prepared to use an intermediary person, such as a mutual friend or member of the family.

◆ Keep a record of your attempts: it will be crucial if you have to go to court.

◆ Keep it simple, and don't make threats of legal action until you are not making any progress.

◆ Be flexible to start with. She may only be prepared to give you limited access at first – accept whatever you get and build from there.

◆ Always make what you want clear, and don't accept a final solution that you are not happy with.

◆ After initial communication has been established, try to get her to agree to go to a mediation service: these professionals are better at getting her to agree to fairer suggestion than you will ever be.

◆ Remember the psychology: she has other motives for not letting you see the kids.

◆ Remember the usual principles of good communication: be open; be flexible and be prepared to ignore some of the insults and accusations that are simply there to fog the real issues.

By talking directly, or indirectly, to her, she will feel as if she is in control. That is a good thing as she will react positively towards it. Many women in this situation want to feel that they have you over a barrel; if so let her – it is not important at this stage. Remember that the *only* thing you need to achieve is access to your kids, and what she gets out of the process is small change considering the benefit to you.

If she will not open a channel of communication or problems still persist after several attempts, and the amount of time you are getting to see your kids does not, in your opinion, allow you to develop the relationship that you want with them, then you have several choices. You can go to court, or allow her to stop your contact with your children. Or you can make a decision to stop seeing the kids yourself – and see if it invokes a change in her reaction.

GOING TO COURT OR CEASING CONTACT

You need to understand the implications of both these actions before you decide what path to take. Don't discount the second choice out of hand. It may be a useful strategy depending on the motive behind the contact abuse. It might also be the only strategy that you can financially afford. If a three-month period of not seeing the kids results in a change of behaviour from your ex-partner, it may be worth the short-term pain for a longer-term gain.

Nobody can tell you exactly what to do in your situation. You must make up your own mind about the reasons for the problems, and then take the most informed course of action. Knowing the implications of your choice is of course key to your decision.

Ceasing contact with your children

Don't disregard this idea – it has some merits.

For example, if your ex-partner has told you categorically that you cannot have any contact with your kids, or that you cannot have the contact period that you think is necessary to develop your relationship with them. If she is motivated by the idea that your kids are better off without you in their lives, then it may be better for you to take some time out, and remove yourself from what could become a very explosive situation.

Many divorced dads who are in this position find that the stress can seriously damage their health. This is also the moment that they are liable to do something that later they will regret. In short, the divorced dad finds himself in a very confrontational situation. And sometimes it is best to walk away – at least for a while.

Stepping back

Walking away at this point is a very non-confrontational approach, which can sometimes be the best way – especially if your ex-partner is looking to get a reaction from you or wants to get some revenge. Again, you need to analyse what her real motive is for not allowing you access to the children. Sometimes stepping back from the adverse situation that you find yourself in gives both of you time to consider what the best course of action is, and allows you time to think about the needs of the children, rather than your own desires.

Stepping back will also send her a message that you are not prepared to fight over the children, and this message alone can sometimes invoke a change in her response. This may also be the best way if, by nature, you are the explosive type and are liable to create some situation which could be used against you in any future legal actions.

Consider this very valid point. By forcing you to take the legal route, your ex-partner can use the legal process to frustrate your access to the children for up to twelve months or, with a good solicitor, even longer. So a three- or six-month period where you step away from all the aggro and heartache, might actually be less time without contact than if you take the confrontational route and fight her through the courts.

Your first instinct will always be to go to court to fight, because you are acting for the kids as much as for yourself. You will feel that you have to do something for the children. You may feel that if you don't take some legal action you are letting the kids down. But fighting your ex in court may be an action that does not serve your children's best interests. This is a time when you need to think before you act.

Benefits

The benefits of stepping away can be immense. You can save a lot of time and money, as well as avoid the stress of having to spend your energy on fighting for contact. Instead you can spend time and energy thinking about how best to become a great divorced dad in the future, creating the space and facilities in your life for your children to grow.

Of course, stepping away might be your only option if you lack the money to take on your ex-partner through what is an expensive and drawn-out legal system. If this is the only option available to you, then you need to make sure you do it the right way, leaving yourself a route back. You will not be alone – many divorced dads find themselves in the predicament of not being eligible for legal aid because they work, but don't earn enough to pay for the cost of going to court (which can run into thousands of pounds).

One benefit of stepping away is more subtle. During this period your ex-partner will not be able to get at you, and she will learn that she cannot use the children as a form of control over you. This may be one of the most important steps in achieving contact with your kids.

Drawbacks

The drawbacks, however, can be a major kick in the teeth. You will miss your children, and during this period they will also miss you. But you must remember that if you are in conflict with your ex-partner, then your contact time would have been minimal anyway, and your short-term pain will hopefully give you longer-term benefits – at least that is what you are gambling on.

Stepping away is a gamble, but there are ways in which you can reduce the odds. There is a right way and a wrong way to step back for a while.

The wrong way is just to stop all contact, with no explanation to your ex or to your children (that is if you can communicate with them). Telling her that you will be back in six months by which time you think 'her attitude will have changed' is a sure fire way of ensuring that she entrenches her position during that time.

Don't spend the next six months moping around and getting depressed; it is much better to develop other areas in your life and make the most of the spare time that you have.

If you don't step away in the right fashion, you can't expect your ex's attitude to change when you do get in touch. But if you do it right you may get longer lasting contact with your children more quickly and cheaply than if you had taken legal action.

The right and wrong way to cease contact

Ceasing contact takes a great deal of courage, because to step away from seeing your children for any period of time is one of the most difficult things that anyone has to do.

But remember this: your children are *your* children, and nothing will ever change that. They will always want to have a relationship with you, as long as you are a kind and loving dad. Nothing will change that; it is in their genes. If you step away for a few months they will still have a desire to see you again, even if their mums have manipulated them.

A child's love goes beyond a few months' manipulation and can withstand losing contact for a short period. It is enduring over time. Whilst they will miss loving you and being loved by you, that love itself will remain and will be there when you return to their lives, providing that you have already given it and of course that you do not abuse it.

If you can communicate directly with your kids, you can prepare them for what is to come and explain to them (as best they can understand) why you feel you need to step way. But don't make the mistake of telling them that you will be back at any particular time. Simply explain that you will be back in contact when the dispute between mum and dad is finished. Tell them that you love them and want to see them as soon as you possibly can.

If you do step away for a period, take time to think through a few matters first:

◆ When you will cease contact.

◆ When you will try to restart contact.

◆ What you will do with your spare time during this period.

◆ How you will communicate with your ex and the children.

◆ What support (family and friends) you will have around you during this period.

◆ What attitude of yours you want to change during this period.

If you are planning to step away for a few months because of the adverse circumstances that you find yourself in, remember that you are *not* abandoning your children, if you are trying to create a situation where you can have contact with them.

How to step away

◆ Send a letter to your ex-partner telling her that you are ceasing contact with her and the children. Don't be tempted to do this face to face.

◆ Do not tell her the real reason – that you think it is a shorter route to getting her to co-operate with you. Tell her you are taking time out to reflect on the current situation.

◆ If possible, speak to your children prior to ceasing contact, and explain in rational – not emotional – terms what you are about to do, and reassure them that you love them.

◆ Do not tell your ex that it is for a set period. Only let her know that you are ceasing contact until the situation improves and that then you will communicate again.

◆ Tell her that, as always, you would love to see the kids at any time, and that your motivation for ceasing contact is simply to allow the current position to change.

◆ Always let her have a phone number where you can be contacted – but don't respond to her calls unless it is an emergency.

◆ Don't tell her family and friends your real intention just in case they go blabbing to your ex-partner. Keep your cards close to your chest.

◆ Try to appear as if you really don't care, especially if she contacts you and tells you that you are abandoning the kids. Your indifference to her emotions will be difficult for her to deal with.

◆ Continue to pay child maintenance – you are not abandoning your responsibilities.

◆ If, when you first make contact again, she refuses, give it more time. Be prepared to be flexible.

◆ When it is time to start again, open a communication channel, and get your ex-partner to come up with a way forward. Let her make the first suggestion.

◆ If she still refuses then get a solicitor and go to court, with the knowledge that you have tried the non-confrontational route.

Remember in all of this to keep a record of what happens at all times. That is why it is so important to put things in letters. Then if it does go to court, you will be able to show that you had good reason for stopping contact for a while.

What will happen to your ex-partner during the time that you don't have contact with her or the children is that she will have the total burden of parenting. She will also have to deal with the emotions of the children who will want to see their dad, and she will also be thinking that you are having the time of your life – free from family responsibility. Slowly these forces will act on her, and she will have time to reflect on her position.

Time is a wonderful commodity – and attitudes inevitably change over time. Where before your ex was bent on conflict, time can remove the strength of her feeling and lessen her motivation. If you handle things in the right way, by using time you can turn the position around. By stepping away from the difficult circumstances you find yourself in, you can:

◆ remove any stress in the situation;

◆ have time to re-evaluate your needs and wants;

◆ have time to consider the children's needs and wishes;

◆ allow raw nerves to heal a bit;

◆ allow your ex-partner time to cool off;

◆ avoid any potential explosive situations;

◆ save money in court fees;

◆ save time in the long run;

◆ let your ex-partner know that you cannot be manipulated.

If you have decided to step away and cease contact, then your ex's concerns at this point will not necessarily be motivated by the needs of the children (or she wouldn't have made contact difficult in the first place). She is probably more concerned about whether she is going to continue to get maintenance from you, and whether you are planning some revenge against her.

If stepping away is to be successful, you must develop some trust in your relationship over the period, and not do anything that would cause her to think that you are going to harm her or the kids. She will already be thrown off balance by your action of stepping away. You must do everything to make her think that you are genuine and that you want to remove conflict from her life, and more importantly the children's lives.

So continue to pay maintenance, and if she contacts you demanding X, Y or Z then give it to her if you think it is reasonable. If the demands are unreasonable, decline in a very peaceful manner, without insult or jibe. If she rings you saying that the kids need some new shoes or other trivial matter, then arrange for some cash to be delivered in an envelope. Don't try and get contact at this point, as you need to ensure that the problems which you were having in the first place are removed first.

Establishing contact with your children after this period needs to be done via your ex-partner. This starts with communication. If that cannot be achieved and you fail to establish a method of talking, then you will never get to a position where you will have unencumbered access to your kids – and you will need to go down the legal road and go to court. But hopefully after a few months' break, which will give emotions time to cool off, and some time in which both parties can reflect on what is most important (the kids' needs) there could be a change in your ex's attitude and she will start to negotiate with you.

If it does not work – or you have decided that the idea of stepping away from the kids is not one that you can contemplate – then you only have one road available to you. Go to court and get a court order for access.

IMPROVEMENTS TO CONTACT ARRANGEMENTS

What improvements to contact arrangements would divorced dads would like to see? An equally good question is what improvements would mums like to see?

The recent DfCA study showed that parents would like the following:

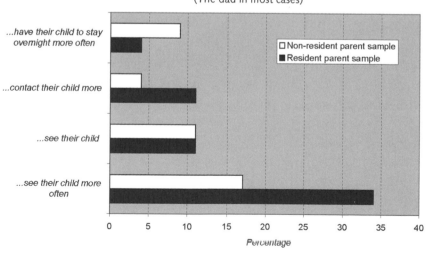

Would like non-resident parent to...
(The dad in most cases)

What is clear from this study is that over 30 per cent of resident mothers would like the fathers to have more contact with their children. This demonstrates the willingness of many mothers to promote better contact for the dad with their children, and can only be positive for both the father and the child.

The reasons for dad not seeing the kids as much as the mum would like are, of course, complex. Some dads don't spend enough time with the kids because they cannot be bothered, whilst others are unable to do so. It may also be the case that some dads disagree and feel that they do spend enough time with their children.

Many parents work together and agree contact arrangements informally. In these cases, improvements can be made quickly and effectively, ensuring that the children benefit from any changes in the adults' circumstances. So in this survey they are likely to have stated that no improvements are needed.

But this is not the true picture because parents who are subject to a court order know they are the devil to change, and making any improvements in a court order means going back to court and going through the whole process again. As such it stands to reason that any improvement needed in these cases will be much more difficult to achieve, leaving fathers and mothers dissatisfied with contact arrangements for a longer period of time.

As well as seeing the kids more often, parents wanted other improvements to the contact arrangements. And the following statistic was revealed – that nine per cent of divorced dads want custody of their children, whereas none of the mums stated it as an improvement.

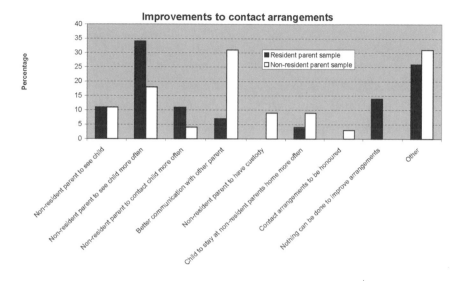

Responding parents of children from the non-resident parent sample reported that custody of the child would improve the contact arrangements (9 per cent) and a small number (3 per cent) said that the contact arrangements being honoured would improve the contact arrangements. None of the responding parents in the resident parent sample stated this as an improvement to the contact arrangements.

What is alarming is that 14 per cent of mothers stated that whilst they were not happy, they did not think that any improvement could be made:

Fourteen per cent of parents of children in the resident parent sample who stated that they were not satisfied with the arrangements, reported that nothing could be done to improve the contact arrangements. All of the responding non-resident parents gave at least one improvement that they would like to see to the contact arrangements.

ABSENT DADS

Not all dads remain in contact with their children. Quite a significant number don't. We know that up to 40 per cent of children lose contact with the non-resident parent within two years of separation, but it is not clear if this statistic includes those men who never started a relationship with their kids – who for some reason were not involved from birth – so it is likely that this figure is a bit higher.

Looking at the overall statistics is a meaningless exercise, because each individual case represents a child who will grow up without one of the two most important people in their lives, and each individual case has its own story. Looking at the overall problem removes the personal pain that many children will feel growing up not knowing, or not involved with, their dad.

The other reason why it is not helpful to concentrate on statistics is that they do not tell us the reasons for the dads' absence. They are fathers who don't stay in contact with their children, but we don't know when it is voluntary and when it is forced.

◆ Is a father who does not see his children because mum won't let him an absent father?

◆ Is a man who does not know that he is the father of the children an absent father?

◆ Is a man who lives away from his children an absent father?

◆ How much contact with his children does a man need to have a year not to be an absent father? For example, if he only sees his kids at school holidays, but is absent for the rest of the time.

◆ Is a man who pays child maintenance but who does not wish to get involved in his children's upbringing classed as an absent father?

Absent dads fall into two categories. Firstly, those who do not wish to be involved in the lives of their children, and secondly those who, for a multitude of reasons, cannot do so. Absent dads are given a bad press which is not always justified. Recent discussions at the CSA about further penalties for absent dads revealed that it is not men who are the biggest non-payers in the absent parent stakes.

In fact the CSA's own research has revealed that 'a marginally higher proportion of women than men refuse to pay child maintenance' (*The Guardian* 10 April 2006).

The CSA's report goes on to reveal that 70 per cent of all absent parents pay some form of child maintenance. This shows that the majority of dads take some form of responsibility for the financial burden of their children even if they don't take an active part in their upbringing.

Other countries (such as Australia) have recognised the long-term emotional damage that the problem of absent parents has on kids, and have put laws in place that enforce both financial and contact arrangements. But here in the UK no such laws exist, although the CSA are being given increasing powers to track down and enforce financial responsibilities on absent parents. However there is currently no intention for any legislation to force absent parents to see their kids, and to develop a relationship (albeit minimal) with them.

There is another side to all this. Dads who don't get involved enough in their kids' lives. Dads who voluntarily only see their children when it is convenient to them and do not consider what is best for their children. Dads who are not 'absent' as such, but take a very peripheral role in their children's development. It is not only the kids who probably want to see more of their fathers – the DfCA study revealed that 30 per cent of mums want the dads to take a more active role and see their kids more often. It is not always the dad who is asking if he can see the kids more often.

CASE STUDY

Not being able to pursue access
Dad: Paul
Child: One son
Situation: Married for 14 days

When I met my partner she already had a child from a previous relationship. That was fine with me – he was a nice kid, and I enjoyed playing with him. The father was not around so I was happy to become his stepdad. We all got on great. I had been going out with my ex for about a year when she told me that she was pregnant. I had not been living with her in her council flat at this stage – well not officially anyway.

We decided to get married (despite my father's advice). It was at this point that life changed. I was married for 14 days before my wife kicked me out of our home.

My ex-wife is not a nice person. It was not until later that I discovered that the only reason that she got pregnant and married me was so she would be eligible for a council house and not a flat. In our area the houses are much nicer, but the council would only give her a home if she had two kids. Having my child for her was all about trading up the property ladder. My dad had tried to warn me about her, but the fact that she was pregnant was a big thing for me as I had always wanted was to be a dad. But with 'I told you so,' ringing in my ears I moved back into my parents' house 14 days after I got wed.

My ex soon started to live with another bloke who turned out to be one of the local hoodlums. He was a bloke you wouldn't mess with, as he had a violent past. When I went round there to try to see my son I was told by him, in no uncertain terms, that if I came anywhere near the place or created any trouble in court, I would find myself severely hurt, to the extent that I would not be able to walk to court.

Given the local reputation of the man, I have had to forgo any contact with my son on the basis of my 'health' being under a direct threat.

My ex-partner has now even changed my child's surname. Now I feel totally isolated, totally unable to do anything about it. It does not matter what rights the court might give me, I need to be able to still be healthy to enjoy them!

So currently I don't see my son. I don't know what will happen in the future, or if my son even knows who his dad is. I can only hope that one day I can meet him when he is grown up and explain how things were to him, and maybe then we might be able to spend some time together.

$$\textcircled{4}$$

Court orders: dealing with the family courts

Suffer any wrong that can be done to you, rather than come here.
Charles Dickens, *Bleak House* 1852

If Charles Dickens had been an observer at the family courts in the last ten years, he may well have made the same comment as he made in his observations of the Court of Chancery in *Bleak House*, set in the Victorian era.

If you are in dispute with your ex-partner and the two of you cannot resolve matters, then your only legal route to obtain contact is to apply to the family courts for a consent order for access to see your children. These orders are also known as family assistance orders. You can only apply if you have, or are disputing, parental rights for the child. Obtaining a court order for contact comes under the provisions of the Children's Act 1989.

THE LEGAL PROCESS

Let's look at the legal process and the approximate costs that a divorced dad has to go through to get a court order for access. Remember that your ex will be faced with similar costs; if parents really knew what the financial costs were going to be, they would probably try to find a way to avoid going to court.

It goes something like this (if you are lucky enough to have an uncomplicated case).

	Action	Time	Cost (approx)
1)	Appoint a solicitor	Two weeks	£200
2)	Apply for a court order	Minimum four weeks before first hearing	£150
3)	First hearing – the judge hears allegations from your ex-partner which may seem scandalous, but are designed to justify her actions and stop you seeing the kids.		£1,500
4)	Judge orders CAFCASS report – a social worker is appointed to investigate you as a father.	Minimum 14 weeks	
5)	Second hearing – the judge reads the CAFCASS report and makes a decision almost entirely on the conclusions of that report.	Another six weeks	£700
6)	Obtain an order – the judge provides you with a defined contact order. This may well be ignored by your ex-partner, and the judge has no real powers to enforce it.		
7)	Several more trips to court to address other issues and breaches of the first order.	3 months	£2,000

Total cost   **£1000s**
Total time   **At least four to five months**
Benefit gained   **Quite possibly none!**

You may be lucky because your ex adheres to the order that you have gained; it may be that because of the cost and aggravation she gives in and stops fighting you. But the likelihood is that going to court will not give you what you want. As the DfCA study shows, the largest area of dissatisfaction for divorced dads is when contact arrangements are ordered by the court.

The study says that the best possible course of action for all concerned is where parents are able to agree informally between themselves:

On the whole, responding parents who had informally agreed the contact arrangements between themselves were mainly satisfied. These parents were less likely to be dissatisfied than by contact arrangements made by mediators or lawyers.

Satisfaction with contact arrangements that had been ordered by a court or negotiated by mediators or lawyers was low, especially amongst parents from the non-resident parent sample. Over half (57 per cent) of the parents of children whose non-resident parent was the respondent and 26 per cent of parents of children whose resident parent responded to the survey and had their contact arrangements ordered by court were dissatisfied with the contact arrangements.

The message is clear – if you have to go to court, you will probably end up dissatisfied with the result. However, it may be your only option; you must hope that you are one of the 47 per cent of divorced dads who end up either satisfied or very satisfied.

Legal costs

It is rare in access disputes for costs to be awarded to either party: so as the divorced dad you should not be liable for your ex's costs – especially if you can prove that you have tried to communicate and be flexible before having to go to court. But at the same time don't think that even though you are in court because she is behaving completely unreasonably that your costs will be charged to her. It simply won't happen.

The first hearing

When you get to court at the first hearing stage your ex-partner, on the instructions of her solicitor, will probably present a series of allegations which are designed to convince the judge that her actions are very reasonable, and that she has always acted in the best interests of her child.

A favourite ploy is to present you or your solicitor with a statement on the morning of the hearing, which has been filed with the judge, listing all the reasons why you are putting your child under stress, and stating that your contact is detrimental to the children. *You must be prepared for this.* The reason that this statement is frequently presented to you on the morning of the hearing is because it does not give you a chance to answer the statement and file a response to the judge.

This statement can allege many things, from something minor like not giving the children enough to drink to something more serious such as violence towards them, or towards your ex. Hopefully the allegations will not be too serious, but it has been known for an ex-partner who really wanted to put the boot in to make up allegations of abuse in order to justify why they wouldn't hand over the kids under any circumstances.

TIP

While this situation is very personal to you, you must remember that it is all part of the legal process. You are not alone in being treated this way.

The allegations used in the statement are designed to make the judge order a CAFCASS (see below) report which is a delaying tactic (it adds three to four months to the legal process and costs your ex-partner nothing). If there aren't any allegations, or any reasonable cause why you should not have contact, the judge is liable to make an order for contact at this point. If this is what your ex-partner wants to avoid, then allegations, which you have to disprove, are made – you must prove that you are innocent before you can have contact with your child.

Don't expect immediate justice – you will be assumed to be guilty of whatever allegations have been made, not assumed innocent as with any criminal offence. The judge will err on the side of caution and assume that there is something to look into, which prevents you from asking him for unencumbered contact at this point in the proceedings.

Unfortunately, this is what happens to many divorced dads, and when it happens it is like a thunderbolt because of the injustice, and the fact that you are powerless to stop it.

CAFCASS at the first hearing
CAFCASS is the Court and Family Advisory Support Service. There is more information about them later in the chapter.

It is probable that a CAFCASS officer (a member of the court appointed social services team) will talk to both parties in an attempt to seek a solution at the courtroom door. However, as your ex-partner is trying to stop contact for a longer term, it is likely that the CAFCASS officer will not make any progress at this late juncture. They can only talk and seek to make a compromise, and it may well not be effective in a situation where views and stances are often becoming increasingly polarised.

You may be lucky and your ex-partner may agree to some compromise at this point – it does happen. It may also be that her solicitor will come up with a series of proposals as a temporary measure. An option considered at this point is an offer of contact at a social services contact centre. This is because your ex's solicitor will not want to be seen as offering no form of contact – and your ex will not want to be instrumental in stopping it. Also, in front of the judge, the solicitor can use it as a negotiating point.

It is up to each divorced dad to decide whether to accept these temporary measures. Whilst it is true that some contact is better than none, pretty much all divorced dads report that contact at these social services centres is in fact a very artificial and depressing experience, which does not enable them to develop a relationship with the child. Also it makes them feel like a criminal, when in fact they have done nothing wrong. CAFCASS however will perceive it as some progress.

CAFCASS appointed to your case

CAFCASS is the equivalent of social services. The appointment of a CAFCASS officer has a very significant impact on any case or court action.

Once the judge has ordered a report then the legal machine grinds – very slowly. In approximately four months the CAFCASS officer will file a report, which will have almost sole authority on what the judge thinks about the case.

During this period it is very difficult, if not impossible, to get access to your kids. If this is what your ex-partner has been trying to achieve it puts her in almost total control of the situation. Whilst you were the person who probably initiated the court action in the first place, it is your ex-partner's tactics that will prevail, and the judge will not give you a court order until the legal process has been completed.

This is why in some cases divorced dads agree to the temporary measures that are negotiated at the door of the court. The 'horse trading' that Mum's solicitor initiates just about sums up the position that you are now in. Your rights (and the rights of your child to see you) at this point are down almost solely to a scrap of an offer that you are almost powerless to improve.

You can always ask the judge to order a temporary arrangement. However, depending on the strength of the allegations that she has made towards you, you may or may not be successful in this request.

Delay at court

Don't be surprised if your ex-partner finds a few ways of delaying the court proceedings if she puts her mind to it. Not being available on the day of hearing (even though she is normally not very busy) or suddenly being ill and not able to attend court, can be ploys designed to delay the legal process. This will result in the system grinding even more slowly – and result in your dispute not being settled over a longer period of time.

GETTING THE COURT ORDER

So you have finally fought your way through the legal process. You have spent hours dealing with solicitors and having to cope with social workers, and spent in excess of £1,500. And you have ended up with a piece of paper which states that you should be able to see your children on certain days and certain times.

This may be enough for your ex-partner to hand over the kids, and certainly for some divorced dads it produces a level of contact with the children. But unfortunately this does not mean the end to contact abuse, as many divorced dads find out to their loss. Just because the judge tells your ex-partner to give you access and allow your children to have contact with you, does not mean that she actually does it. The biggest failure of the Children's Act 1989 is that it does not have any teeth, and if your ex decides not to adhere to the terms of the court order there is practically nothing that the judge can do to enforce it.

You may find that instead of you achieving good quality access to your children, the people who benefit from your experience in court will be the solicitors who always get paid, no matter the result to their client. You, on the other hand, have been dragged through a stressful experience, accused of many atrocities, spent a lot of money and many hours in unproductive time – with very little result.

You must adopt an approach which is designed to draw up a fair and workable court order which will benefit the kids, and be flexible enough to avoid breakdown at the first hurdle. In short, you need to consider what you wish to be defined in a contact order – what time you will be able to spend with the kids and how it will be a template to giving you the time to develop the meaningful relationship that you strive for.

What can be included in a court order for contact

When drawing up a contact order, you should consider all of the aspects of child contact. This includes the following:

◆ times and hours of contact;
◆ stay-over arrangements;
◆ transport arrangements;
◆ rights to have contact for holidays;
◆ special days (eg Christmas and birthdays).

The proposed order should set out clearly what the arrangements for the children should be. It is worth noting that under the Children's Act 1989 it is the child who has the right of contact with the father; the order is drawn up for the benefit of the child and not the parent. So whilst it is the divorced dad who applies for the order, the judge will make the order out for the benefit of the child. The fundamental philosophy behind a contact order is that it is designed to protect the right of contact for the child; it is the children who have the right for unencumbered access and not the parent.

A workable court order

The purpose of going to court is to obtain a court order which gives a child a schedule of times and dates for contact with the divorced dad. It regulates contact and ensures that there is time provided to establish and develop a positive and loving relationship. The court order needs to be workable from several people's perspectives: the dad's, the mum's, and the child's. It needs to be workable for all parties if it is going to be successful. It is no good for the order to be drawn up favouring one side or the other – each party must approve it, or the order will not be adhered to. As enforcement is a real problem, consent is the only way in which an order can be made to work.

Under the terms of the Children's Act 1989, court orders for access are supposed to remove problem areas, and protect the rights of the children to have contact with both parents. A properly drawn up contact order will go a long way to achieving this, as it can set out a fair and flexible schedule for contact times. Court orders are made up with the assistance of independent people (CAFCASS and the judges), and backed by the authority of the law. That is the principle.

TIP

Contact orders can be an excellent tool for divorced dads to use to ensure a continued presence in their children's lives. They can be used to create a framework for the time and space in which to see the children and enjoy and plan a life together.

It will involve, and specify, time. Time is the most valuable resource and without enough of it, it is impossible to be involved in any aspect of the child's life. But equally, you need to realise that you have to create a life outside the role of dad. There is a need to ensure balance, in order to build happiness in your life. There is no point in drawing up a contact order that takes up all your free time, as you need to develop your own life as well as your relationship with your child. As your children get older, they will want to have more time to themselves, outside of the contact with either parent. Contact orders need to recognise the maturity and independence of the children and their needs as well as the needs of the parents.

The key to making a court order for access work is to build in some flexibility, whilst respecting all the key issues. If you obtain an order that is too rigid, then it will not be long before your ex-partner breaches the terms of the order, which will lead to contact abuse and a return to court.

TIP

Contact orders need to be draw up with flexibility and fairness, or they simply will not work over time.

A second principle in drawing up a workable contact order is fairness. If your ex-partner does not think the order is fair to her, then she is likely to ignore the terms in that order very shortly after the judge has made it, leading you back to court for enforcement. There she may well make up a series of allegations or reasons why the order is unworkable, and force you back into the legal cycle from direction hearing to CAFCASS report to more hearings – during which time she will not adhere to the terms of the original order. It is best in the first place to draw up an order that can be agreed to by you both.

Keeping the contact order flexible

◆ Try to set out minimum times rather than specifics. For example, 'five hours on a Sunday' is better than 'between the hours of 10:00 and 15:00'.

◆ Try to set minimum notice periods for any changes, for example four weeks' notice of when the kids are away on holiday.

◆ Try to set out alternatives. If the children are not available on certain weekends for example (maybe they are on holiday or away for the weekend), then have an arrangement that within 21 days the contact times are made up.

◆ Remember that you are not available every weekend, so build in some flexibility for yourself. If, for example, you are not available for the stated arrangements then you will suggest three alternative arrangements for your ex-partner to choose from, and provide reasonable notice.

The more flexibility you can build in the more likely you are to get a workable order and you will end up with more contact with your children. This fact is simple, but so relevant. The more defined your contact order is, the more opportunity your ex-partner has to breach a part of the order – and then ignore the rest of the terms of that order.

The downside of this is that contact may not be on a regimented basis, and you will have to work more closely with your ex-partner in order to make contact work. If you are not able to do this because of your poor relationship, then you need to be prepared for her to breach the terms of the order on an increasing basis, as she discovers that there is not much you can do about it and not much that the judge will do either.

TIP

Workable court orders can be drawn up, but the best scenario is to use the court as a platform from which to build.

You may find that what you agree ends up being for the convenience of your ex-partner, as she may take advantage of your desire to spend time with the kids, and will give you more time when it suits her. But this is a small price to pay for the pleasure of seeing your children.

If by being flexible, your ex-partner gets to benefit, then it does not matter, as your children will benefit more from the time that you will spend with them. If your ex-partner takes complete advantage, then you still have the terms of the basic order which you can stick to, or try to enforce; if it has been drawn up correctly, will have a degree of fairness built in.

Changing the terms of a court order

If you want to change the terms of a court order for access then it can be done in two ways. Firstly you can get an agreement with your ex-partner, and make the changes on a voluntary basis. If this is not possible, the second option is to return to court and vary the order. This is fairly straightforward, and involves the same process as applying for the order in the first place.

If the changes are uncontested by your ex-partner, then there will be no CAFCASS report or investigation, and the judge will make out a new order at the first hearing. However, if the changes are contested by your ex-partner, then the full process of CAFCASS reports – directions hearings and further hearings, along with arguments and time in front of the judge, will apply. This is why it is important to draw up the order in the first place as best you can and build flexibility into the terms of that order.

Breaching a court order for access

There will be times when you cannot adhere to the terms of the court order that you have. Maybe you have to go away for a weekend training course at work, or you have another commitment that precludes you from spending your allocated time with the children.

The key thing is to recognise that it will happen (although hopefully not too often) and try to agree a formula with your ex-partner which can accommodate such circumstances. Firstly, let your ex know it is going to happen – and also the children if they are old enough to understand. You don't want them building up their hopes of seeing you on a certain date if you are going to be elsewhere. Secondly, you must try to offer alternative times to both your ex-partner and to the children. It is also best to offer several alternatives as they themselves may have other commitments.

You must never think that you have a right to breach the order. It was drawn up for the benefit of the child, and gives you an obligation to be there 100 per cent of the time. Of course, this won't happen in the real world, and if you cannot be there, ensure that you offer your ex some times that are suitable. If no time can be found, then there is little you can do other than forfeit your contact time.

Failure to either communicate or offer alternatives will probably be used against you should your ex-partner want to return to court and get the order amended, so it is always best (in cases where there is a hostile ex) to write a letter or send an email as proof of communication and an alternative offer. Be reasonable, and hope for the best solution. Where your ex-partner is not hostile, you should be able to work out an alternative contact time to see the kids, but be pragmatic as you might need to give a little ground (maybe in agreeing to collect and drop off the kids) in order to make it happen.

CAFCASS

The impact that CAFCASS will have on your court application will be immense, and any divorced dad who is going through the court process will need to have a thorough understanding of the pitfalls and procedures of dealing with these court-appointed officers. The more you can learn before coming into contact with CAFCASS, the better positioned you will be to get a reasonable solution from the court case.

Failure to understand how you will be treated, and failure to know what the procedures are, will lead to a disaster for any divorced dad who is subjected to a CAFCASS investigation.

TIP

Any divorced dad who gets involved with a CAFCASS officer needs to know what he faces.

CAFCASS is a branch of the social services, and a CAFCASS officer is a social worker in disguise.

They are appointed by the court to investigate your child's welfare. Their role is to look at the overall welfare of the child or children, and investigate any allegations made about you by your ex. They then produce a report and make recommendations to the judge about a suitable level of contact. These recommendations will be taken by the judge (increasingly without question) as the preferred course of action.

What each CAFCASS officer does is to produce a report which is designed to consider all the facts in a balanced way, and come to a conclusion with recommendations for the child. It is the recommendations of this report that are now frequently taken by judges as the best possible solution for the child. The CAFCASS officer is seen as an independent arbiter between the parents and a person who will look at the case from the point of the child's rights. Hence a lot of weight is placed on the conclusion and recommendations of the report.

The CAFCASS report is sent direct to the judge prior to the court hearing, and each parent also receives a copy.

Preparing the CAFCASS report

As with many branches of the social services, much depends upon the individual skills of the social worker in deciding what the issues are in each case. Therefore a basic part of the report process is the expertise of the officer who is making it. CAFCASS literature will tell you otherwise, but the experience of many divorced dads is that CAFCASS officers vary in their ability to get down to the real issues.

Each CAFCASS officer has to follow a procedure laid down by the service, to eliminate individual bias and gain as full a picture as possible about the child's welfare. The interview procedure follows these steps:

Step one
The CAFCASS officer interviews both parents separately, and starts the investigation into any child welfare issues raised (typically by the mother) during the court case. They also listen to any other issues that either parent wishes to bring to the attention of the CAFCASS officer which have not been raised at court. The first meeting is mostly done at the offices of the CAFCASS officer.

Step two
The CAFCASS officer interviews the child in the presence of the father. Many dads allow this to happen at the offices of CAFCASS, which is a mistake as they cannot feel at ease or relaxed in the environment of the offices.

TIP

Remember that you don't have to have your CAFCASS interview in the office. Ask the officer to come to your home.

Step three
The CAFCASS officer interviews the children at the mother's residence, in the presence of the mother. Depending on the age of the children, a series of questions is used. For younger children (under eight) a picture book can be used, the CAFCASS officer might ask the child to draw pictures to describe their family, their

feelings and to draw a picture of their parents. A few divorced dads have reported that children can feel intimidated by this and they think that because they are being interviewed in mum's house it can be biased towards the resident parent.

Step four
The CAFCASS officer interviews the child independently – sometimes at the CAFCASS offices.

Step five
In addition to the interviews, the CAFCASS officer writes to the child's school and seeks input from the head teacher on the child's welfare.

When all the interviews are complete, the officer will produce a report on the child's welfare and on any issues that have come up during the investigation. The report will follow a standard format, which is as follows.

1. Summary of the action taken by the CAFCASS officer in compiling the report.
2. Background information.
3. Notes on the interview with the applicant (normally the divorced dad).
4. Notes on the interview with the respondent (normally the resident mother).
5. Notes about the child's concerns.
6. Welfare checklist, split as follows:

◆ the ascertainable wishes and feelings of the child concerned (considered in the light of their age and understanding);

◆ the child's physical, emotional and educational needs;

◆ the likely effect on the child of any changes in their circumstances;

◆ the child's age, sex, background and any characteristics which the court might feel relevant;

◆ any harm which the child has suffered or is at risk of suffering;

◆ how capable each of the parents, and any other persons in relation to whom the court considers the question to be relevant, is of meeting the child's needs.

7. Conclusion and recommendations.

The report is designed to record the findings of the CAFCASS officer accurately, and is structured in such a way that will lead to a set of conclusions and recommendations. It is the intention of the CAFCASS officer who is producing the report to come up with a series of recommendations for the child. And many of the headings of the report are designed to consider the situation from the perspective of the kids. This is of course in keeping with the Children's Act, which seeks to protect the right of the child to have contact with both parents.

CAFCASS recommendations

The final section of the report is a series of recommendations. These are centred around what the CAFCASS officer believes to be the best course of action for the welfare of the child. They recommend what level of contact there should be, where that contact should take place, and how it should be managed. In short, unless both parents have found some agreement during the process, the CAFCASS officer makes the suggestions that the court will adhere to. These recommendations are supposed to be independent and neutral, serving the welfare of the children.

CAFCASS officers (in their own departmental guidelines) are supposed to keep both parents abreast of their thoughts as the investigation progresses, so that the recommendations that they make do not come as a great surprise to either party. These recommendations are then submitted to the court. However, many divorced dads do not know that they have the right to be kept up to date with the thoughts of the officer concerned. As a result they don't ask about the conclusion until the final report is written and already presented to the judge.

TIP

Phone the CAFCASS officer and ask questions such as:

◆ When are the interviews?

◆ What are his/her thoughts?

◆ Where is the officer in the process?

The recommendations are supposed to be rigorously questioned at the next court hearing by both parents (or by their solicitors), and where there is a conflict of opinion, a decision imposed upon the parties. At the end of the procedure, an order is made which is adhered to by both parents, for the benefit of the children.

But the whole CAFCASS report process and practice is subject to many flaws. Many divorced dads feel they are disadvantaged; they find that instead of producing a fair and balanced report, the system adds to the bias which already exists in the legal process. Instead of helping to gain good access to the children, it is in fact an opportunity for the resident mother to block still further contact with the children.

CAFCASS – the real position for divorced dads

A simple search of the internet reveals many documents that have been posted by divorced dads who have been subjected to the injustices of the CAFCASS service. There are several organisations (such as the Equal Parenting Council) which have sprung up as a result of poor and inappropriate reports produced by CAFCASS officers. These poorly-produced reports have led in to a reduction in contact for fathers with their children. A search across newspapers (available online) reveals many other cases of divorced dads who have not received a fair hearing from CAFCASS.

The truth of the matter is that CAFCASS – as an organisation – is not up to the task of deciding contact arrangements for parents. CAFCASS is loathed by many divorced dads, and has been found to be lacking in the appropriate skills and resources for the job that it has to do. This is not just the opinion of organisations such as Families Need Fathers or other dad-centred groups (nor the opinion of many of the fathers who have been subjected to the injustice and inefficiency of CAFCASS) but by independent bodies reporting directly to the government.

A report to the Parliamentary Select Committee (October 2003) severely criticised the CAFCASS organisation and made over 45 recommendations for change. At the time this damning report led to the resignation of the chief executive of CAFCASS services.

Many people have concerns about CAFCASS, such as:

◆ CAFCASS officers very often lack any formal training and qualifications; they often have a probation background and are unused to dealing with cases like these.

◆ There is a very limited complaints procedure, and complaints are dealt with within the organisation.

◆ CAFCASS keeps no records on the outcome of cases that they have handled, and as a result has no way of knowing if the best outcome, for children and parents, has been achieved.

The most frequent complaints made by divorced dads about CAFCASS are:

◆ CAFCASS officers appraise each case on the basis of getting a solution with the least possible conflict; as a result sometimes there is very slow progress on contact issues for the dad.

◆ In many situations, CAFCASS officers do not try to substantiate any lies that they are told by the mother, but accept them as the truth. In many cases CAFCASS officers make a record of the allegations and include them in their reports.

◆ CAFCASS officers are not trained enough to differentiate when the children have been manipulated by the resident mother into making statements or showing emotion that are contrary to their own thoughts and feelings. Sometimes they cannot properly assess the independent views of the children, and place too much emphasis on small children's views which have in fact been put on them by the mother.

◆ The officers are often biased towards the mother to the extent of not really listening to or following up claims of the dad; they are more concerned with keeping the resident mum happy and engaged in the process.

◆ When the child is interviewed with the mum it is generally at home, which allows the child to be relaxed and be natural. Whereas when the child is interviewed with the dad it is often at the CAFCASS office, and not in a natural setting.

◆ Some dads report that it seems their CAFCASS officer has so much work that they seem disinterested in the case in front of them.

Dealing with a CAFCASS report

Reading reports or talking to other divorced dads should help you deal with your CAFCASS officer. In addition, there are some basic rules which all divorced dads need to think about:

Avoid conflict and anti-social behaviour
CAFCASS officers will be told by the mum about any incident that has created conflict between the parents, and any incident where you have lost your temper with her, especially if this was in front of the kids. If there are any incidents of violence or otherwise, then the mum is likely to tell the CAFCASS officer that this is harmful to the emotional wellbeing of the children.

Unfortunately the CAFCASS officer may well ignore the fact that you lost your temper because your ex-partner refused to give you access to the children in the first place, and conclude as a result of the violence your contact with the kids is stressful to the child and mother and should therefore be curtailed.

Avoid:

◆ violence to the mother;
◆ violence to the children;
◆ anti-social behaviour.

Beware that the officer won't always verify the truth and sometimes accepts the mother's word that something has taken place. If you are questioned about such instances then be prepared to have a point of view that is balanced. Also if you did, in fact, act in a violent manner, make sure that you can persuade the CAFCASS officer that it will not happen again and that you realise the effect that it can have on the children – make it clear that you regret what you've done.

Interview with dad
Always ensure that your focus is on the children's needs and not your own. When interviewed, ensure that you came across as:

◆ flexible;
◆ child centred;
◆ non violent;
◆ considerate to your ex-partner.

Remember to back up any statements with facts and evidence. This is the time to produce the diary of events that you have been keeping, and the record of phone conversations and/or letters and emails.

Interview with you and your children
When the CAFCASS officer wants to interview you with your child, they may well want to do this at their office. If you can, ask

to do the interview at your home, where your child will be more relaxed. Ensure that the officer stays for more than 30 minutes, and just be natural with your children. If you can, get access to your child an hour before the CAFCASS officer arrives, so that they can relax and lose any negative influence that the mother might have tried to have on them.

School report

If your children are at school, the CAFCASS officer will approach the school. Make sure you have spoken to the children's head and class teachers and taken an interest in the development of your child's education. The CAFCASS officer needs to know that you are interested in the wider welfare of the your child.

Proposals

Make proposals to the CAFCASS officer, but ensure that they are reasonable and designed for the benefit of the children. Try to make proposals that the CAFCASS officer can take back to your ex-partner and see if she will agree. Most CAFCASS officer would like to get an easy solution – so if you can come up with some proposals it avoids them having to do the thinking themselves.

Golden rules for dealing with CAFCASS officers
Do ...

- ◆ **co-operate.** Try to come across as a really flexible guy who is interested in achieving a solution.

- ◆ **think of your children's needs first.** Be child-centred – state your arguments from the child's perspective.

- **be respectful towards your ex-partner,** even if she isn't towards you. You must show that you understand her position, and understand that you have to create a working relationship with her if things are to progress.

- **remain calm and relaxed.** CAFCASS officers deal with divorced dads each and every day. They want an easy life – don't give them any reason to think that you are a problem.

- **stay focused on what happens next.** Don't get bogged down in discussions about the past – try to focus on tomorrow and what happens in the future.

- **compromise.** Recognise that you won't get all that you ask for and be prepared to make compromises in order to move on.

- **communicate.** You need to ensure that you communicate openly to the officer – if you come across as guarded they will think that you are hiding something.

- **think long term.** When making suggestions try to put forward long-term plans which will improve your relationship with your kids (and make sure they are plans you can deliver).

- **think about other members of the family.** Work out how they can help, and how the kids can benefit from contact with them.

- **spend enough time with them.** Get all your points across.

- **prepare.** Think before you meet them about what to say and what to do.

- **provide evidence** of any matters that can promote your case.

- **remember** that this is an investigation – the officer is determining if you are an OK father.

Don't . . .

◆ **slag off your ex-partner.** You will come across as bitter and twisted, and the CAFCASS officer is likely to see this as an area of added stress for the child.

◆ **be confrontational.** You will be seen as a trouble maker.

◆ **be obsessed with your children** – you need to come across as a balanced parent.

◆ **be defensive** – you have a lot to offer your child.

◆ **be rigid** – you have to be flexible in your proposals.

◆ **accept any old rubbish** that the CAFCASS officer tries to accuse you of. Ensure that they back up any negative statements about you with facts.

◆ **focus on your needs.** Contact is the children's right and your presence in their lives is for their benefit not yours.

◆ **come up with unworkable proposals.** They will waste time.

◆ **put yourself first** – for obvious reasons.

◆ **be aggressive or argumentative** with the CAFCASS officer. They have the ultimate sanction.

◆ **skip it** – you need to spend time and energy with these social workers.

◆ **think that a CAFCASS officer can tell** if your ex-partner is lying. They can't, so ensure that you resolutely defend any spurious claims made against you. Expect your ex-partner to make up some counter claims which harm you, and don't expect the officer to be able to see them for what they are.

- ◆ **try to be a smart arse.** The officer is a human being and won't take kindly to be proven wrong.

- ◆ **expect your ex-partner** to tell the truth, or to come up with any proposals. She may well not.

CHILD GUARDIANS

If a case drags on in a lengthy court battle, a judge may ask CAFCASS to consider appointing a child guardian in cases where there are some complex and ongoing issues over contact with the divorced dad. These child guardians are appointed by the court to represent the rights and interests of the children. What it means is that the child will be represented by their own solicitor in future court hearings and also represented by the presence of a child guardian (normally a CAFCASS officer).

Child guardians can only be appointed under a rule of law and only by a circuit judge or higher. In other words, it is beyond the powers of the magistrates at the family court to appoint a child guardian. The case must be referred to county court and above.

Child guardians are there to help achieve the best possible outcome for the child they represent – they advise the court about what needs to be done before it makes its decisions, and write a report for the court saying what they think would be best for the children. This report includes the wishes and feelings of the children. To do this the guardian spends time getting to know the children and members of the family. They may also recommend to the court that other professionals are asked to help, such as child psychologists.

TIP

Child guardians always consider the wishes and feelings of the children, and their report will say what they think is best, although this may not be the same as what the children want.

The court will take very careful note of the instructions of the child guardian, and in the vast majority of cases will rule based on their recommendations. As with CAFCASS reports, the document is sent to court, as well as to the parents, and the guardian attends the final hearing at court and can be questioned about the findings.

Divorced dads' experiences of child guardians shows that much depends upon the individual capabilities of the guardian in determining the right outcome for the child and father.

The court may also order support organisations such as Pro-Contact (a charity which provides formally supervised contact for families), or local children's charities to get involved in your case, if the judge feels that it would benefit the child or contact arrangements. These are additional hurdles for the divorced dad to overcome, but in the medium to long term child guardians may assist fathers to have more access to their children.

Sadly, for a lot of divorced dads going to family court, obtaining a court order is not the end of their woes. The major problem with the family courts is that the court does not possess the power to enforce its own orders. In other countries – notably the USA and Australia, the court that issues the order can impose a penalty on a parent who does not adhere to the terms of the order. In

Australia, a step approach is taken to penalties – starting with fines, moving to community service and (only in severe cases) prison.

In the UK the family court is extremely limited in its power. It only has one sanction, which is prison, and this punishment is almost never used because it affects not only the mum but also the child. In short, when Mum breaches the contact order, the only thing that the family court can do is to give her a telling off, which seldom works, or is taken on board.

So divorced dads are forced to spend time and money in their initial struggle to get proper contact with their children, in a court which ultimately cannot give them what they set out to do.

FROM THE FAMILY COURTS TO COUNTY COURT AND BEYOND

In the UK a divorced dad has to work his way through the family court and then show good cause as to why the case should be transferred to the county court. For the average divorced dad this could mean up to ten separate hearings at the family court.

The reason this is such a protracted affair is because mums and their solicitors have become adept at dragging things out. Involving CAFCASS, making up allegations that then need to be disproved, and agreeing to a court order at court – and then ignoring it. Whilst all this is going on your access to your children is limited – if not non-existent, and it is costing you time, money and causing a significant degree of stress.

It is no surprise that some divorced dads give up on their struggle to see their children, as they simply cannot afford carry on with the legal process. Of course, one way to reduce costs is to represent yourself, and this is a course that many divorced dads take. If you are not confident enough to represent yourself, then you can enlist the help of a Mckenzie Friend (see page 150).

Eventually, in the worst cases the case is transferred from the family court to a higher court. At this point, everything becomes more expensive – should there be a contested hearing your ex will probably use the services of a barrister, and you may have to do the same. By this time the CAFCASS reports are inches thick, and probably several in number. Most divorced dads have been to mediation a couple of times, and the court papers can be stacked feet high on a desk.

It is unlikely at this time that there is any substantive reason for the dad not being allowed to have access to his kids, as it would have been discovered by CAFCASS or the court prior to this time, and dealt with. So for most divorced dads arriving at county court there is no real reason why they should not be given the access they want to their children.

TIP

At county court, judges are far less tolerant of mums who are blocking access simply because they are the resident parent.

So if the problem is simply one of contact, then moving up to the county court normally provides the solution, as the judges are far more likely to impose an order on the mum. This is well known among solicitors, who finally advise their clients accordingly.

However, if your dispute is more complex than just contact – perhaps for example you are trying to get shared or sole residency of the kids – then if the matter is not settled in the county court, or the decision is subject to an appeal, your case can be taken right up to the House of Lords. In practice, very few divorced dads get this far, because they either get a settlement earlier, or run out of steam in their fight to get their rights.

It is also not in your ex-partner's interest to take matters this far. However, her circumstances may be different – she may not be working, and so can get legal aid, costing her nothing. It may also be difficult for your ex to back down at this point. If she has been telling the court that you are Attila the Hun (even through the CAFCASS report has been telling the court that you are a decent bloke) she may have been telling the lie for so long that she has come to believe it herself.

So moving from the family court up to the county court is, for some divorced dads, a vital step in either getting some form of contact or another necessary step in getting some residency rights. The best course of action is, of course, not to have to go there at all but to seek a solution before incurring the costs and time that is involved with going through the courts – in other words mediation. But this is not always possible, so divorced dads have no option but to continue their personal struggle against the system.

TIP

Remember that giving up the fight means giving up on your children, and in years to come they will be thankful that you did not give up, and that you continued to fight for their right to have unencumbered access to you.

HELP IN COURT: A MCKENZIE FRIEND

What is a Mckenzie Friend?

Many divorced dads cannot afford to retain the services of a solicitor, and end up representing themselves at court. This is not as difficult as it first seems, but what can be of real help if you are going to represent yourself is the assistance of what is known as a Mckenzie Friend.

The name comes from a particular case, Mckenzie v Mckenzie (1971), which established a legal precedent and gave everyone the right to use a friend as an assistant in court. The original case was in fact a divorce case but the principle in law is the same for family cases, and it has been tested right up to the court of appeal.

So any divorced dads caught in today's legal process can use a friend as an assistant in court. This is usually someone who is a mate or acquaintance of the divorced dad. They have gained knowledge of the court system and procedures, probably by having been involved in the family courts themselves.

The Mckenzie Friend has the right to attend court, to take notes, and to quietly make suggestions to the divorced dad, whilst proceedings are taking place. Although they have no right to actually address the court, in some instances the judge will allow them to. This can be very useful to any divorced dad who is not very good at speaking up for himself.

The right to have a Mckenzie Friend in court is now well established, in England at least. Whilst they have no legal status, you have the right to whatever assistance may be reasonably required – and that is the basis for allowing a Mckenzie Friend in court.

CASE STUDY

A Mckenzie Friend
Dad: William
Child: Ellie (aged two when separated)
Situation: Not married. Separated for five years.

Since my separation over four years ago I have hardly seen my daughter. Despite having been told by CAFCASS and by an independent mediation service that I should have unsupervised access to my daughter, I have seen my daughter barely more than three or four times per year.

I started with a solicitor who was fine, but he couldn't do anything other than adhere to the law and represent me accordingly. The problem has been that every time I have used him it has cost me a fortune. I have probably spent in excess of £5,000 in solicitor's fees. I don't earn much, about £17,000 a year, so I couldn't afford to keep him. But I didn't want to drop the court case because if I did my ex-partner would never give me access to Ellie.

A good friend of mine had also gone through a rough time so over a beer I asked him what he would do. We had a long chat about the case; luckily I had taken with me a lot of the court papers, so we had the information that we needed to hand. I explained that I simply could not afford to carry on and that the bank would not lend me any more money. I asked him if he thought that there was anything else that I could do.

At first he asked me if I had thought about representing myself which I had, but my problem is that I am not a confident person, and didn't feel able to do this. Then he mentioned a Mckenzie Friend, and after we had talked about it he agreed to become my Mckenzie Friend.

He helped me file the proper application forms at court, and to prepare the statements. My ex-partner had never come across a Mckenzie Friend so her solicitor had to explain to her what it was all about. He treated my Mckenzie Friend just the same as he had treated my old solicitor.

Although at court officially my Mckenzie Friend could only sit near me, take notes during the proceedings, and offer me advice in the form of whispers, many judges in fact allow Mckenzie Friends to do the actual talking. I knew I would be tongue tied speaking to a judge so I prepared a statement asking if he would allow my Mckenzie Friend to speak for me on my behalf.

The judge was great – he realised from the way in which I read my statement that it would be the best thing. And he allowed my Mckenzie Friend to speak for me.

Since that first hearing I have been back to court seven times (in front of seven judges – all of whom have allowed my Mckenzie Friend to speak for me). Without this assistance I would have really struggled to carry on.

Using a mate as a Mckenzie Friend has not only been great in court but has also helped me keep up my motivation to carry on. There have been a few moments when I have felt like caving in and dropping the whole thing, but the moral support has kept me going.

To be able to speak to another divorced dad who has shared some of the problems has been fantastic, a real help, and has enabled me to carry on my court battle at no cost. We both agree that a solicitor may have been able to get slightly quicker progress – but given that I could not afford one, I am grateful for the progress that we have made.

I am still fighting. My ex has just about run out of reasons for not letting me see my daughter. She has tried lots of things to stop me having parental responsibility. She has attacked me on child welfare matters – telling the court that I could not look after a three year old (despite the fact that I have another child two years younger and I am a care worker), as well as refusing to attend several courses of mediation.

She has thrown childhood illness and allergies at the court as well as the kitchen sink. During this time I have remained calm (even if inside I am hurting like hell). And all this time she has had a solicitor which must have cost her in excess of £10,000, and still counting . . . I have often wondered why her solicitor keeps representing her as he must know that she will eventually have to comply with a court order. But then solicitors get paid irrespective of the result or the time it takes.

What a Mckenzie Friend offers

If you are going to use a Mckenzie Friend you should try and find someone who:

♦ gives his/her time freely (they are not allowed to be paid);

♦ has some knowledge of the family court and the people who appear in it (such as CAFCASS);

♦ has time to come to court with you;

♦ has time to help you in between court hearings with the paperwork and putting together your defence.

If you do not know any one who has the experience or time, then pop along to your local branch of Families Need Fathers (see 'Useful Contacts' at the back of the book) and ask at a meeting if there is anyone who can act as your Mckenzie Friend. You should find people who are willing to help you.

The benefits of using a Mckenzie Friend are immense. Not just on the days in court, but also helping you to prepare and process your case. You can save thousands of pounds over the term of your proceedings by not using a solicitor, and by utilising a lay representative. For many divorced dads this means that they can continue in their fight to gain decent levels of contact via the courts. Because a Mckenzie Friend is not a solicitor you cannot get the same level of legal advice – which does slightly hamper your case – but if the choice is whether you can afford to carry on with your battle through the court or not, then using a Mckenzie Friend can help you.

The benefits of using a Mckenzie Friend are:

◆ help with the paperwork – they may well know what forms are needed and how to prepare them;

◆ help in your defence – they will be able to provide guidance and advice in helping you prepare statements for the court;

◆ help on the day – some judges will allow them to address the court;

◆ they can take notes and offer suggestions during the proceedings;

◆ they can give you moral support: be a shoulder to cry on as well as someone to talk to.

Many divorced dads cope with representing themselves, without the help of an assistant. But if you can find someone to help, then it is certainly worth it. Even if that person cannot attend the court dates, they can help in the preparation of your case and ensure that you serve all the relevant court papers on time, and to the right people. But probably the biggest help is the moral support. Having someone around to talk your case through – someone who understands what you are faced with – is of tremendous value. It might even help keep you sane!

Letting the court know

If you are going to use a Mckenzie Friend in court then it is best to inform the court in advance. You can do this by completing a simple letter to the judge. It is polite to send a copy of this letter to your ex-partner's solicitor as well. By doing this you avoid any questions on the day, and it may well help to allow the Mckenzie

Friend to speak at court (should you require it) – if no objections are made by your ex's legal representative.

The letter you send should look something like this:

In the   Court

Case no:

TO: The clerk of the Court
DATE:
REF: Mckenzie Friend

Dear Sir/Madam

At the hearing in the aforementioned matter before the court on _____ it is my intention to represent myself with the assistance of a Mckenzie Friend.

In order to avoid unnecessary delay on the day of the hearing, please place this letter before the court and confirm that there is no objection to my having such assistance or provide reasons for any refusal.

Yours faithfully

(Litigant in person)

Address for service_____

References:
Collier v Hicks [1831] 2B & Ad.663
Mckenzie v Mckenzie [1971] p 33

The attitude of your ex-partner to you representing yourself will range from indifference to hostility. She may well not have come across the principle of having a lay representative at court, so will have to find out from her solicitor about Mckenzie Friends. She cannot object to it. If she has been trying to wear you down, and hoping that you will get to the point where you cannot afford to fight her any longer, then your new tactic will give her the message that you are prepared to go on fighting until a resolution has been found.

In short – if you are planning on representing yourself at court (because you have either run out of money or lost patience with your solicitor) then using a mate as a Mckenzie Friend can be of significant help in your efforts to act for yourself.

CASE STUDY

Representing yourself in court
Dad: Jason
Child: Maisie (aged three when separated)
Situation: Jason and his ex were not married. They lived together for six years.

After mutual agreement, my ex and Maisie left the family home and went to stay with her mother. Initially there were no problems and I was able to see Maisie when it suited us all. I would simply phone up and arrange a time to pick her up. I did not have her for overnight stays as my ex would not allow it, which was not a surprise to me as she was always very protective towards Maisie, even to the extent of not letting her grandparents take care of her during her first few years.

However, four months later – at exactly the same time as my ex cleared out her things from the family home – I was stopped from seeing my daughter. No reason was given beforehand. I rang, but got no answer. I could not understand what was going on, so I went round to see her parents. Her mother, who I had never got on with, had great pleasure in basically telling me to get lost (in not such polite words). She would not tell me where my ex or daughter were, nor how to contact them – only that I was not wanted in my daughter's life.

I was dumbfounded and did not know what to do. I felt helpless, but I had no idea that it would be a long-term problem – I thought that it would be resolved in a few weeks. I was very much mistaken.

I reflected on the last four months – had I done anything wrong? I didn't think so. I had always treated my ex with respect, always looked after our daughter when I saw her, and always paid my child maintenance, even buying extra things along the way (shoes for nursery, and an extra coat for playing out).

I thought that whilst living with her parents my ex might have been influenced by her mother. If only I could get to talk to my ex, then surely we would be able to communicate and find a resolution.

But despite my best efforts to contact her, it did not happen, so I had to go and talk to a solicitor. That was three and a half years ago, and I have now been to court over 10 times. At no point in these proceedings has my ex ever given an explanation as to why she has become difficult over access.

When I first went to court I used a solicitor to help me, but in all honesty I felt as if I never got great value for money. I spent over £3,000 in fees, for very slow progress. I never seemed to get the chance to ask for what I wanted in court. Each time we arrived at court the same process would take place. Her solicitor and my representative would talk together, come back to me and my ex, then haggle a bit more, and reach some form of agreement which was never what I expected or wanted.

I was always told that this was the 'best deal' on the day, and that 'in order to move it forward' I should agree. Then the solicitors would go in front of the judge, inform him that both parties had an agreement and ask him to agree the deal. I would leave court with some small step forward, but never really understanding why I could not get what I wanted.

At this point money was getting a bit tight, but I did not want to stop my court action. So I read up on some websites about fathers' rights, and sent a letter to my solicitor informing them that I would represent myself. Having been to court at least five or six times by then I knew roughly what to expect, but I was very nervous. I had observed what my solicitor had done and tried to copy him. I wrote a detailed statement before I went into court (copying the format of ones that I had done for the case previously) and arrived at court.

The first time I had to do it on my own was hard – I had to remember to keep the statement factual, without attributing blame: I focused on the what/when/how rather than the why. It was key to stay focused on Maisie's needs – the needs of the child are the only thing that the judge should take into account. I remembered to always talk about Maisie's rights to see her dad rather than my right to see her.

When I got to court the officials were a bit shocked that I was representing myself. But I have to say that it has been a great experience – I was finally able to tell the judge directly what I thought and what I wanted. I would recommend that any divorced dad who has to go to court represents himself if he can because the judge is actually there to help. My judge was excellent – helping me understand what would happen next and telling me what paperwork I needed for the next hearing.

I really felt as if I could represent myself better than any solicitor because I really cared about my daughter – this was not just another case but my child's future.

All in all it took me about eight hours to prepare for each hearing, compared with about £800 for each time I got the solicitor to represent me. I reckon that I have saved thousands of pounds since, as well as knowing that I have been able to do my best.

I am delighted to say that at that point I started to make great progress and was able to get a court order which gave me access to Maisie. Over the last three years I have been able to build on each small success. The first order was for three hours a week, the next for six, and then for a complete day. I agreed with the judge to review these after every three months, and every time I went back to court I got a bit more!

My ex-partner did not always comply with the court order – she would often tell me that Maisie was ill or did not want to come. I took a relaxed attitude to this because I did not want to rock the boat; I would simply look forward to the next weekend when I would see her. I then returned to court and got a written court order for access to Maisie over a complete weekend – including overnight stays.

And since that point I have not seen my daughter at all. It has been over six months now, and despite no reason being given by my ex, other than that my daughter does not want to, I have not been able to communicate with her about the next step. I guess that I will have to go back to court and get another court order.

In all honesty I have lost a lot of heart. Maisie is now six and I have to make a decision whether to return to court or to do nothing and let Maisie grow to an age where she can decide what to do.

I think I will get back to court and carry on with the case – it won't cost me anything (financially) but it will take a lot out of me in terms of stress and emotional energy. Maybe one day, when Maisie is old enough to make her own mind up about whether to come and see her dad, it will all be worth it. At times I lose the will to carry on but luckily my family support me, especially my new partner. And even though having to go through the whole legal process has left me bitter and resentful to my ex and her family I still love my daughter more than the pain and stress than that causes. So I guess even if it goes on for the next eight years, I am resolved to carry on trying to get a fair deal for Maisie.

5

Mediation services

It is obvious that where there is a dispute between parents, some sort of compromise is needed if the matter is to be resolved. Unfortunately, if dad and mum are not speaking – or at least not respecting each other's views – then somebody else has to become involved if a solution is to be found. This can be achieved in several ways, either by a judge imposing an order on the parties (which they are disinclined to do at the outset) or by trying to find a compromise outside the courts. This can only be achieved quickly with the use of a mediation service.

Mediation services can either be professional, or in the case of minor disputes where the matter has not yet gone to court, a trusted friend can be used to negotiate a settlement between the parents. Parents can choose to use any mediation service voluntarily – but in reality very few parents do. In most cases the use of a mediation service is ordered by the court if the judge feels that the parties can resolve their disputes away from the court process and get an agreement with the use of this professional service.

In the UK very few couples who are separating use a mediation service until problems develop. They tend to assume that mediation is not required at the outset, and that they should be able to resolve any minor disagreements between themselves without the involvement of other parties.

For many divorcing or separating couples this is indeed the case, and mediation services are never required, as the parents co-operate together and compromise accordingly. Unfortunately, sometimes one parent (very often the mum) does not co-operate and respect the other's position, and so communication breaks down. The unco-operative parent has to be brought back to the negotiating table by using a mediation service.

TIP

Before going to court to achieve a court order for access, suggest to your ex-partner that you use a mediation service as a better way of getting a solution to the problem.

The dad is already in a weak negotiating position (as he is in most cases the non-resident parent), and mum controls most of the affairs relating to the child. Also inherent in this process is the fact that the people at the mediation service are the parents – the children are only represented through their views – which does not necessarily mean that the children's thoughts and wishes will be uppermost in the parents' minds when they sit down with the mediator. It takes the mediator's skills to bring both parents around to acting on the best interests of the child.

The good news is that mediation services are staffed by experts. The mediator is adept at being neutral, and seeks to resolve matters from a neutral standpoint. They also consider matters from the standpoint of the children, and in most cases approach the case from the view of the child's wants and needs, given their experience of working with children in this environment.

The bad news is that most mediators will not suffer parents who are not prepared to compromise, and are quick to terminate mediation if they feel that no progress will be made towards a solution. In short, the mediator will not waste their own time and energy on a case where progress will not be made.

If mediation breaks down, the reasons for the breakdown are not put in a report which can be submitted to a court. So if your ex-partner is intransigent, and is dragged towards mediation by the court but fails to take the process seriously and the mediator terminates the process, she will not be disadvantaged. The mediator's report will not state that she failed to take an active part in the process – only that the process broke down. It will not say which party was the cause of the breakdown.

MEDIATION: FAQs

Is the purpose of the mediation to get dad and mum back together again?

No. Mediation is for couples who have separated, or are in the process of separating or divorcing. It offers the chance to talk about, manage and resolve issues arising from the breakdown of the marriage.

How do I go about organising mediation?

In two ways. Firstly, if you decide to go to mediation voluntarily with your ex then you can use the mediation services of an organisation simply by contacting them and setting a date for the first meeting – but this will cost you money. Or secondly, in matters of dispute over contact, you can get the court to appoint mediation (normally after a CAFCASS report) – in which case it costs you nothing.

What sort of people are mediators?
Mediators are in most cases professionally qualified or have other qualifications, eg as solicitors, counsellors or CAFCASS officers.

How long does mediation take?
Generally it takes between two and eight weeks to set up the first meeting with the mediator. They then progress matters fairly quickly, with weekly or fortnightly meetings between the parties, each usually lasting one to one and a half hours.

How long does mediation last?
Generally, mediation sessions can resolve the issues (if possible) within three to five sessions.

Is an agreement made at mediation legally binding?
No, although the summary prepared by the mediator once mediation is complete can be given to your solicitor to be incorporated into a court order or a legally binding agreement. But this is not the case if mediation is appointed by the court and breaks down.

Is mediation confidential?
Mediation is a confidential process. However, most mediation organisations reserve the right to notify the relevant authorities if the mediator feels the child is at serious harm. They also have a legal obligation to report any suspected fraud, such as benefit fraud, tax evasion or undeclared money.

TIP

At the mediation sessions, ensure you are flexible and focused on your child.

AVAILABILITY AND CHARGES

Mediation services are provided by organisations such as

◆ the Family Mediation Service
◆ NCH – the children's charity
◆ other local children's charities.

See 'Useful Contacts' at the back of the book for more details.

These organisations are neutral and can be used outside of court. If you can get your ex-partner to agree to use a mediator, then both of you can go along to the service and start the process. However this will cost you money as only court-appointed mediation is free of charge.

The charges are typically based on your earnings and are a sliding scale. Compared with the alternative, which is having a solicitor represent you at court (and all the time and stress that goes with it) it's probably quicker and cheaper to get an agreement via mediation.

TIP

Think about volunteering to pay for mediation as your ex may well be sceptical of your motives. If you volunteer to pay it will be cheaper than a solicitor's costs in the long run.

If you can persuade your ex-partner to participate in a mediation service, you give yourself a chance of getting a solution to your problems over contact/access in the quickest possible manner. As it is done in a neutral way as well, your ex is more likely to stick to whatever agreement the mediator can negotiate.

If divorced dads who end up going to court could turn the clock back on their own court battles then they would instigate a mediation service at the outset, as it can resolve matters prior to things becoming even more polarised at the court. But it is important to recognise that mediation does not work in all circumstances, and in cases where mother is resolute that she will not openly and freely discuss matters, and respect the opinions of either the negotiator or the divorced dad, then mediation will fail. In these circumstances, the only option left to the father is to obtain a court order.

THE FUTURE OF MEDIATION SERVICES

In a perfect world, at the slightest sign of a dispute all divorcing couples would be made to go to mediation to resolve matters, and those recommendations would be binding on both parties. Unfortunately, we do not live in that perfect world. But there is a growing feeling that mediation services could be more widely used in family courts. A recent report to the Lord Chancellor addressed the issue specifically (a full copy of the report can be found at www.dca.gov.uk/family).

The report considered the use of a mediation service in cases where fathers were having problems in getting access. Although the report recommended some important changes, it did not go far enough. Various fathers' rights organisations continue to argue and debate about more radical changes, but the fact remains that using mediation is not compulsory, nor are the recommendations of that mediation legally binding on the parents. Until these changes actually become law, then mediation will remain a tool that can be used by divorced dads to help the process, but is a blunt object in getting justice for them or their children.

6

Your financial responsibility to your children

Every divorced dad is faced with some major decisions about child maintenance. The fact of the matter is that separation or divorce changes dramatically the financial situation for both parents. For most divorced dads the early days of the separation is a very expensive time, with the costs of setting up a new home and paying for legal fees, as well as trying to maintain a level of income for his ex to support their children.

The resident mother has to do without the earnings of the father coming into the house. With the much-published CSA regulations, the mum can now calculate in advance how much she will receive when you are no longer resident in the old family home. In all likelihood this will mean a severe drop in her disposable income, even if she has a job herself.

Financially, divorce or separation is a nightmare and very few parents are better off in the early days of their separation. The financial balance changes and remains changed until the child is of an age when maintenance is no longer payable (how old depends on how long the child stays in education). For most divorced dads, the idea of paying child maintenance is not a problem as they recognise their responsibility to contribute to the costs of the children.

Many dads, however, have a problem with the level of payments, or the fact that they cannot control that the money is actually spent on the children.

TIP

Under current UK law, whether payments are made under a CSA order or under a court order, divorced dads do not generally have the right to ensure that monies paid to the mother actually go to the benefit of the child.

It is the responsibility of the resident parent to ensure that the child's needs are met, and the dad's responsibility is to pay an amount which contributes to those needs.

The facts are simple. Whatever money was in the family pot before separation and covered the costs of running the family home now has to go much further, and cover the costs of running two homes – one for mum and the kids, the other one for dad. Obviously, with these additional expenses, standards of living for all parties are going to drop, and sacrifices have to be made in order to balance the books.

If the parents were married, as part of any divorce settlement financial matters are hammered out between them, and at some point a decision made about the family home, and any other family assets. Once the settlement is decided upon it will be ratified by the court. Part of that settlement will be a decision about ongoing child maintenance: whether to have a court order for periodic payments (child maintenance) or to allow the issue to be handled by the CSA.

In the case of a couple who were not married, and therefore did not go through a divorce process, these matters are almost inevitably handled by the CSA, unless you have managed to reach a voluntary arrangement with your ex.

THE SHIFT IN ECONOMIC BALANCE

When you set up home somewhere else there is an income shift. Not only are you now paying your own additional costs, but you are also making payments to your ex-partner for child maintenance. This puts severe pressure on most dads and sacrifices have to be made. In general, up to 25 per cent of a divorced dad's income goes to his ex and the children. Of course, your ex has to make sacrifices too; as she now cannot rely on the income that you used to bring into the family home.

The effect on the dad of this shift can be dramatic – especially when you consider that the CSA does not consider the mother's income, nor any income her new partner might have, relevant. This can lead to a significant imbalance in the economies of the two parties – the mum and the dad.

In the UK most mums work, and whilst there is still a difference between what men and women get paid and the hours they are able to work, many mothers enjoy a significant salary. Society tends to be sympathetic to the plight of the mum; the media and many feminist groups will tell you how difficult it is for divorced mothers to maintain a lifestyle comparable to what they had before they were divorced. But if finances are hard for mums, consider the dads' plight.

CASE STUDY

Mr Jones and Mrs Jones are divorced. They have two young children. Mr Jones is a store manager earning £25,000 a year, and Mrs Jones is an estate agent on £20,000 a year.

Mr Jones pays 20 per cent of his net earnings to Mrs Jones, as per the CSA guidelines. Mrs Jones lives in the old matrimonial home as part of the divorce settlement.

	Mr Jones	Mrs Jones
Monthly gross income	£2,083	£1,666
Tax + national insurance + pension	£ 430	£305
Net monthly income	£1,653	£1,361
Child maintenance payments	– £290	+ £290
New monthly income	£1,363	£1,661
In addition		
Mrs Jones gets child tax credit and child benefit		£100
Mr Jones has additional living expenses, and Mrs Jones has childcare costs	– £200	– £200
REAL MONTHLY INCOME	£1,160	£1,551

So now Mrs Jones only has access to £1,551, instead of £3,115 (previous combined income), Mr Jones' position is worse with his income now dropping to £1,160.

Stories in the media which report that only mothers are less well off after a divorce are misleading, as they ignore the income shift between the parents and discount the new economic position faced by fathers. The harsh reality is that divorced dads find themselves in a position where there is a major economic change which can only be met by a reduction in their lifestyle. This shift leaves many divorced dads without enough money to live on.

Society tends to focus on the divorced mother's financial position after separation, and not to see the father's. It is very difficult for a mum to pay all the bills with her £1,551, but also it is much more difficult for the divorced dad to do so with only £1,160.

One thing is for sure – whatever the exact income shift, there are very few couples who feel as if the other has contributed as much as they should, and finances remain an area of conflict between separated parents.

Money issues in divorce – as in marriage – are, as many relationship counsellors can testify, symptomatic of power struggles between the parties. The laws of divorce and the CSA claim to be geared to fairness and reason. Yet from the divorced dad's point of view the results can be quite unfair, especially when he has no control over what the money is spent on. It is no surprise then that many divorced dads seek to minimise their child maintenance payments and look to get the best possible deal from the courts or the CSA.

CHILD MAINTENANCE: THE OPTIONS

You have three options when it comes to child maintenance (not including the separation of the family assets as part of the divorce settlement, which is a one-off financial agreement but covers ongoing child maintenance).

The options are:

◆ court order for periodic payments;
◆ CSA;
◆ a voluntary agreement with your ex-partner.

There are major differences between each option, and you need to consider which will be the best deal for you. This is not only in the short term – child maintenance is due until around when a child is 19 so the long term must also be considered.

It may not be a choice that you get to make as your ex-partner also has a right to decide which route to go down, and the choice may be made for you. In which case you need to learn quickly what is in store.

A recent study by the DfCA revealed that:

Over half (56 per cent of both samples) of all maintenance agreements were made informally between the child's parents. Around three in ten maintenance agreements were made through the Child Support Agency (28 per cent of children in the resident parent sample and 30 per cent of children in the non-resident parent sample for whom maintenance was paid). Slightly more than an eighth of each sample had their maintenance agreements made through a lawyer or a court (14 per cent of children in the resident parent sample and 13 per cent of children in the non-resident parent sample for whom maintenance was paid). One per cent of children in each sample had had the maintenance payments made by their non-resident parent agreed through the Family Mediation Service.

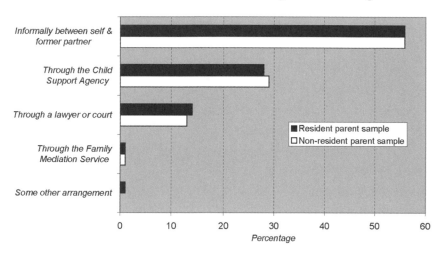

How maintenance arrangements were agreed

What this study shows is that there is a need for almost one in two divorced couples to have the children's ongoing financial arrangements decided on by a third party (CSA, court or other). Only about half of parents can agree it between themselves.

THE CSA

Much has been reported on web pages and said in pubs and bars about the horrendous experiences of divorced dads who have been subjected to an investigation by the CSA. A good search of the internet will reveal many tales of how men have been left penniless through the actions of this government body; and if you are interested in the history of it then you can go on a search engine and read about all the tales of woe.

Established with the goal of getting absent parents to pay for their children, the CSA was quickly used by mothers as a way of getting increased contributions from dads who were paying what child maintenance they could afford. Statistics have proved that the CSA has been a worthless exercise, with the costs of the organisation far outstripping the benefit to the tax payer. Any dad who, prior to 2003, had to endure an investigation by the CSA, found himself embroiled in the worst case of government bureaucracy and came out of the process with less money than he needed to live on. This was because the guidelines for assessing child maintenance were so clearly wrong. It resulted (after many headline cases and a great deal of social injustice) in the principle rules for assessing the amount of child maintenance changing dramatically in early 2003.

At this point, in 2003, a new set of rules was applied to new cases that are assessed by the CSA. This makes the CSA a much friendlier and fairer option to divorced dads than prior to 2003, where the only piece of advice to a separated dad would have been to avoid the CSA wherever possible.

The CSA process

Any parent who has residency of the children can ask the CSA for an assessment if the following conditions apply:

◆ the child or children are under the age of 19;
◆ there is no court order for periodic payments.

If a couple were not married, but the father's name is on the birth certificate, then the CSA is also used by the resident parent to make a claim for child maintenance.

Who is entitled to apply for CSA assessment?

Any resident parent (or in the language of the CSA a 'parent with care') – normally the mum – who has residency of the children can ask the CSA for an assessment if the child or children are:

◆ under the age of 16;

◆ between 16 and 19 and in full-time non-advanced education (this means that the child is doing a course not higher than A level standard).

If the child lives in Scotland the rules are slightly different – if over 12 they can apply for child maintenance and a variation in their own right.

In addition it is not only mums who can apply to the CSA – dads can too. Non-resident parents can also start their applications for a fair assessment through the CSA.

Working mums
Mums who do not get income support or income-based job seekers allowance get to keep every penny of any CSA-assessed child maintenance payments. Also, any CSA-assessed child maintenance has no bearing on their child tax credits – so there is nothing for working mums to lose by applying to the CSA for an assessment.

Mums receiving benefits

Any resident parent who currently claims income support or job seekers allowance is automatically deemed to have made an application to the CSA by means of their state benefits – unless she has opted out. She can only opt out if she feels that there is good cause of a risk of harm either to herself or the children, or undue stress, in which case the father will not be pursued as part of the claim.

In cases like this, as part of the process there is a home visit by a clerk when the case is discussed, and if it is felt that a risk exists, the dad will not be sent the paperwork to be made aware of the claim. This opt out is to protect women who have violent or harmful ex-partners, and is useful for women who fear retribution if their ex-partners are pursued for money to pay for their children.

In cases where the mum refuses to give the name of the dad, and she does not demonstrate good cause, then the penalty for her is that her benefits are reduced by 40 per cent of the income support or job seekers allowance.

If the mum is on state benefits then she doesn't keep the cash that the CSA collects from the dad. The CSA keeps up to £10 per week, which is known as the child maintenance premium. So in practice, if your ex-partner is on state benefits then she is foolish to go to the CSA if you are giving her more than £10 per week, as she will not directly benefit. However she might feel as if the money is no good in your pocket and make a claim anyway, in which case you will lose and the government will gain as it is the exchequer which keeps any extra cash claimed from you.

When the CSA cannot get involved

In addition to the situation where there is a risk of harm or distress, there are other circumstances where the CSA has no jurisdiction.

The CSA cannot accept an application for child maintenance if there is:

◆ a written agreement between the parents of the qualifying children, made before 5 April 1993, for the non-resident parent to pay regular child maintenance;

◆ is a court order for periodic payments made before 3 March 2003, which says that the non-resident parent must pay child maintenance for the qualifying children;

◆ a court order made on or after 3 March 2003, which says that the non-resident parent must pay regular maintenance for the qualifying children, and the order has been in force for less than a year when the application is made.

In addition, the CSA cannot accept applications if the non-resident parent lives abroad (although there are some exceptions if they work for an employer who is based in UK).

What happens when the mum applies to the CSA

The mum is interviewed by a clerk and completes a form which provides the CSA with the information needed to process the claim. This interview is actually done at their home (where possible). The completed maintenance administration form is passed to the CSA who then contact the non-resident parent and seek child maintenance.

How child maintenance is worked out

In order to calculate how much you might need to pay in child maintenance, it is important to get to grips with the language and terminology that the CSA uses.

NRP	non-resident parent (generally the dad)
PWC	parent with care (generally the mum)
WFTC	working family tax credit
Qualifying children	children for whom the NRP has to pay child maintenance
Relevant other children	A child who is living in the same family as the non-resident parent. This could be a child of the NRP or the child of another person living with the NRP.
Voluntary payments	Payments made to the PWC for the benefit of the child prior to an assessment being made.
Shared care formula	A formula to recognise that the NRP has costs of looking after his children during his contact.
IMA	Interim maintenance assessments

The basic formula

There is now a simple formula that the CSA uses to work out how much the NRP will pay. This formula is designed to be relatively simple and based upon a degree of fairness and equality.

The formula is based on four criteria:

◆ the NRP's net income (see below);

◆ the number of qualifying children that maintenance is due to cover;

◆ the number of nights of shared care;

◆ the number of relevant children (children in NRP's household, including step children).

Net income

The net income starts as your gross income, including any bonus payments or other benefits that you get in your wage package. Then all income tax, national insurance and contributions to pension schemes are subtracted. This new figure is then used as your net income. The formula ignores all net income above £2,000 per week, so if you are in one of the four per cent of divorced dads who earn in excess of £100,000 per year your maintenance is capped. But for the rest of us, all net income is taken into effect.

If the household claims a tax credit such as WFTC, then the amount of the tax credit that is treated as net income is:

◆ if the NRP is alone or earns most, 100 per cent;
◆ if the NRP's partner earns most, 0 per cent;
◆ if they earn the same, 50 per cent.

The CSA can find this tax credit information from the Inland Revenue directly, and in fact the CSA rules talk about 'who earns most at the time of the tax credit claim' to ensure this.

Number of qualifying children

This part of the formula is obvious, as it is based on payments according to the number of children that need maintenance. Quite logically, it is a sliding scale:

Number of qualifying children	Basic payment for maintenance
1	15 per cent of net income
2	20 per cent of net income
3 or more	25 per cent of net income

If you have one child that you need to pay maintenance for then your payment is 15 per cent of your net income less any allowance for shared care and other qualifying children. The most you have to pay – if you have three children or more – is 25 per cent of your net income, as CSA payments are capped at 25 per cent of your wage.

If you earn under £200 per week, there is a separate calculation which means that you pay less than the above amounts. This is an attempt by the CSA to recognise that divorced dads need a basic amount to pay for their bills and living expenses, so as to not put you in the poverty trap. For dads who are themselves on income support or job seekers allowance, the minimum payment currently stands at £5 per week.

CASE STUDY

Tony and Jane are divorced and have two children who both live with Jane. Tony is required to pay 20 per cent of his net income of £220 per week in child maintenance because he has two children. His maintenance is therefore £44 per week.

Relevant other children
If you have children living with you in your new family home, the CSA takes it into account when assessing child maintenance for the kids who are not resident with you. Interestingly, the children

living with you do not need to be your own. If your new partner has children, then they also qualify.

The net income is reduced as follows:

Number of relevant other children	Net income is reduced by
1	15 per cent
2	20 per cent
3 or more	25 per cent

CASE STUDY

Stephen and Nicola are divorced, with one child who lives with Nicola. Stephen lives with his new partner Sarah and their two children. Stephen's weekly wage gives him a net income of £280. Because he has two children living in his current family home, his net income is reduced by 20 per cent (£56) before his child maintenance is worked out. His child maintenance should be 15 per cent (because he has one child living with Nicola). His payment is worked out as £280 less £56 = £224 x 15 per cent, which leaves him paying £34 per week.

Shared care – if children stay with their fathers
An allowance is made by the CSA if a child stays overnight with you on a regular basis, and the amount of money that you will have to pay is reduced in line with an addition to the basic formula. This is worked out on the basis of how often you look after the children during the week, and is designed to recognise the costs incurred in looking after the kids at this time.

The way that the reduction is worked out is as follows:

Number of nights of overnight care by the dad per year	Child maintenance for the child is reduced by
0–51	Zero
52–103	1/7th of the amount assessed
104–155	2/7th of the amount assessed
156–175	3/7th of the amount assessed
175 or more	1/2 of the amount assessed

These overnight stays do not need to be set out in a court order; they are simply the nights that you have had your child. It is vital that you keep an accurate diary of the time that your kids spend with you, as you can produce this as part of your assessment and reduce the amount you will need to pay in child maintenance.

CASE STUDY

Stephen (see previous example) normally pays £34 per week. He looks after his child twice each month (for a long weekend), for two weeks in the summer, a week at half term, as well as four nights at Christmas. This makes a total of 74 nights a year. So Stephen's child maintenance is reduced by 1/7th, leaving him to pay £34 – 1/7th = £29.

Special costs
You can ask the CSA to take into account any special costs that you have in relation to your children. These can include any of the following (although it is not an exhaustive list):

◆ any high costs related to seeing your children, eg travel costs;

◆ extra costs because a child in your care is disabled;

- a debt incurred before the separation (providing that the debt was for the benefit of the family);

- boarding school fees;

- the mortgage or insurance on the family home that you no longer live in.

The basic formula revisited

The formula for child maintenance assessments could therefore be stated as:

Percentage of dad's net income (15 per cent for one child/20 per cent for two children/30 per cent for more), minus:

- allowance of shared care;
- allowance for qualifying children;
- allowance for any special costs.

Multiple children with multiple mums

This is where the basic approach to the formula starts to get a bit more complicated (because life generally is!).

The rules and regulation for the CSA get a bit more complicated in cases where the divorced dad has several children by more than one mum. In CSA language this is a multiple case.

The formula that they use is based on common sense, and divides up the money that the dad has to pay amongst the mums who need it. Child maintenance is worked out for all of the qualifying children the NRP has to maintain. The amount is then divided between the parents with care in proportion to the number of children they have living with them from the dad.

CASE STUDY

Jim is the non-resident parent of Ruth's daughter Tracey. He is also the dad of Jill's sons Kevin and Tony. He is separated from both of them.

Jim is required to pay child maintenance for three children in total, so that is 25 per cent of his net weekly income of £360 – £90.

The amount is divided between his two ex-partners in proportion to the number of children, and each of them gets 1/3rd of £90 for each child. So he gives £30 to the mother of his daughter, and £60 to the mother of his sons.

If a PWC makes an application for child maintenance from more than one NRP, the child maintenance due from each NRP is calculated separately.

Where to get information about the CSA

The best place to get information about the CSA is to download the info packs that they have on their website: www.csa.gov.uk. There you can find a series of leaflets that you can print out. Some of the best ones are:

◆ Child support: A technical guide (CSL109)

◆ Child support: Your child maintenance interview (CSL 100)

◆ Child support: A guide to how child maintenance is worked out (CSL 102)

◆ Child support variations: Help for exceptional circumstances (CSL 108).

Refusing to co-operate

Can the CSA penalise you if you don't co-operate? The simple answer is yes. If you are a PAYE taxpayer the CSA can get the information they need, so there is little point in delaying matters and incurring penalties.

Changes in the new CSA formula include penalties and punishments. It is a criminal offence under the child support law if you:

♦ fail to provide information when the CSA requires it;

♦ give information that you know is false.

The CSA will make an order for you to pay a default amount in the case where they cannot or do not get the information that they want. These default amounts are:

Number of children	Default amount (per week)
1	£30
2	£40
3 or more	£50

The CSA can impose a financial penalty for failure to pay (under the reformed system), as an incentive for people to pay the full amount on time. (The CSA doesn't need to do this if there is a good enough reason for the failure, and penalties can be appealed.)

These penalties can be up to 25 per cent of the liability, so failing to pay (say) £40 in a particular week may result in a penalty of £10 for that week. This penalty is not part of the child support payment (which remains due). The penalty goes to the Treasury.

Also, the CSA needs to go to court to exact the penalties as they themselves cannot impose them.

Punishments

These punishments came into operation early in 2001 and apply to all cases, not just those under the reformed system. Courts can impose the following punishments if the person concerned is found guilty of the following:

◆ **failing to provide requested information** when available, or knowingly telling lies: a fine of up to £1,000;

◆ **consistently failing to pay the required amount of child support maintenance**: loss of driving licence for up to two years, as an alternative to prison, and only after other means have failed. The court should take notice of whether the driving licence is needed for making a living.

Default maintenance decisions

These are to ensure that money starts flowing as rapidly as possible to the resident parent, even before enough is known to do the proper calculation. They replace IMAs. The default payment (per week) is simply £30 for one child, £40 for two children, and £50 for three or more children. These default maintenance payments are standard. It is always a sensible thing to pay these amounts voluntarily, as it will have no negative effect on your wallet when the assessment is completed.

If the later calculation is higher than this, the extra is due (as arrears). If it is lower, however, there is no refund. (There are also 'interim maintenance decisions', which applies where a 'variation' has been applied for and a proper decision cannot yet be made.)

Trying to avoid the CSA

If your ex-partner is not receiving state benefits
If she is not receiving benefits, she will not automatically come under the CSA's jurisdiction and the best way to avoid the CSA is to come to an agreement with her. Sadly, for most divorced dads, that simply is not feasible as some degree of animosity exists (post separation) between them and their ex. In fact, your ex-partner may consider that she can cause you a significant degree of upset by applying to the CSA, especially when she learns that she has nothing to lose, even if she does think that you are paying enough towards the costs of the kids.

If your ex-partner is receiving state benefits
In this case, it is almost impossible to avoid being contacted by the CSA (unless you give your ex-partner good cause to show that she is at risk or under stress). You really only have a couple of options: you can leave the country (but then you would not get to see your children and build a relationship with them), or try and stall the process in order to give yourself a bit of time to prepare your case.

In truth, if you want to stall the CSA then you need to ensure that they have no possible way of contacting you. In order to do this, you need to hide your address and contact telephone numbers from your ex-partner. The reality is that this is very difficult if you are still having contact with your children, as your ex-partner needs to be able to speak to you to sort out the arrangements for the kids. So unless you are planning on doing a bunk, and not seeing the children, then it will be virtually impossible for you to remain undetectable to the CSA.

Minimising the payments

The question that most divorced dads ask is not how to avoid the CSA, but how to minimise the amount of money that they give their ex-partner. In other words, how can they get the lowest possible CSA assessment? They feel this especially as they have no control over how their ex spends the money, or even if it goes towards the children in the first place. Many divorced dads are angry that the cash they give does not seem to be spent on the kids, and feel they should keep some back and then spend it directly on the children in the form of activities or other expenses, so as to ensure that they get the benefit of their earnings.

For the vast majority of divorced dads having to pay a 'professionally assessed' child maintenance payment is not a problem – they recognise their responsibility towards contributing fairly to the upkeep of their children. For some divorced dads, however, the situation is not so straightforward and mums make contact dependent on paying cash. These fathers would love the opportunity to go to the CSA and pay the assessed amount, rather than the amount that the ex-partner decrees.

However, for a quiet life (and for the opportunity to build their relationships with their children), some divorced dads agree to pay the ex-partner what they demand. Blackmail does exist – and in these cases divorced dads have very little that they can do. They either choose to pay out the increased amounts or don't get to see their children.

TIP

If you are on PAYE earnings you have little reason to avoid the CSA. Certainly, it is true that the CSA represents the fairest yet method of assessment, and at least is formula driven, so dads can be assessed in a uniform and controlled way.

The new formula used by the CSA is increasingly seen as a fair way of setting child maintenance. The CSA guidelines are increasingly used by court when making periodic payments orders, so in reality most divorced dads are no longer worse off by having a claim against them handled by the CSA rather than by any other organisation.

Minimising your CSA assessment
If you accept that it is right and proper for all divorced dads to pay a level of child maintenance, then being assessed by the CSA will, in principle, be a fair way to calculate the payment. However, many divorced dads seek to minimise the amount that they hand over to their ex-partner so that they can have some money left to spend on the kids themselves. It is difficult for many fathers to manage financially, as they have extra bills at this time, so many divorced dads seek to keep as much money as they legally can in their own pockets.

A lot of divorced dads need to ensure that they are not paying more than they have to, and want to minimise the cash that they will have to pay. This is worthwhile considering. If you can save yourself £10 a week in child maintenance, it adds up over the year and subsequently over the lifetime of the child. £10 a week (after tax) equates to £520 a year – for most dads that is in excess of £700 per year in gross earnings.

To put it in context, that 'saved' money could pay for you and your children to go on a holiday. So think for a minute about the great fun and experiences you could give your children if you can minimise your CSA assessment – something you might not otherwise be able to afford. Or think of the fact that the £10 per week could pay for the activities that you do during your contact time; it could pay for a trip to the cinema, or put petrol in the car so that the kids can have a trip out to the countryside. Or even pay for a bag of chips at the seaside. In short, the father can ensure that the money goes to the benefit of the kids.

If you would like to minimise your CSA assessment then you need to consider how to:

◆ minimise your net income;
◆ maximise your shared care allowances;
◆ maximise other allowances;
◆ claim for extra costs.

Minimising your net income
There are 97 per cent of the population working in normal jobs, and get their earnings automatically processed by the organisations that they work for through the PAYE system – so it is not possible to hide any gross earning that you have. But there are things that you can do.

◆ **Don't do any overtime** during the period of the assessment. It will be taken as your gross earnings and an assessment made including 'optional' overtime.

- **Increase your pension payments,** as this will reduce your net income. You can always reduce your pension payments after the assessment.

- **Make sure that any bonuses** you get are not paid out during the time of your assessment.

- **If you are self-employed,** consider an offshore company for some of your earnings.

- **Pick a time when your earnings are lowest** when asked to provide evidence. This is normally for three months.

- **If you work for a small firm,** talk to your employer and see if he or she can help you out with any temporary agreements to minimise your wages. Only what is on your payslip during the period of the assessment is counted.

Maximising your shared care allowance
You can save a lot of money by ensuring that you maximise your allowance for the overnight stays that your kids have with you.

- **Pick your kids up on Friday teatime** (for the weekend) rather than Saturday morning as it adds extra time to your assessment and reduces your liability.

- **Keep a diary** of the nights that you have them and ensure that you claim for them all.

- **Try to have your kids overnight** during the week at school, as for a little time you can save money.

- **Make sure that you count up** holiday times for the summer and Christmas.

◆ **Look at the formula:** if you are close to a break point, then try to get the kids for an extra week in the school holidays or for an extra night at weekends so as to get your time into the next break point.

Maximising other allowances

You may not have any other allowances for step children, so this might not be applicable. But ensure that you include any other children that you have or any children that live in your household in the assessment as the effect can be dramatic on your final payout.

In addition, make sure you claim for any loans that were taken out during your relationship, ensuring that you state that they were for the benefit of the children (a good reason is to pay for a holiday, or credit card debt built up during your relationship).

Other expenses

You are better to apply for any of these to be taken into consideration, and let the CSA refuse your claim, than not apply for them at all.

◆ You can apply for travel costs to pick up your children.

◆ If you are picking up your children and you live a long distance way from them, you can claim to have your hotel costs taken into account.

Other things that you might try in order to make the assessment a more difficult process for the CSA are:

◆ Stall the process by not giving the CSA a telephone number and making them write to you about everything – the money is better in your account than theirs.

◆ Take your time in replying to letters and requests for information, about 28 days is the maximum, unless you state that you have been on holiday or likewise.

◆ Stop paying when your child is almost 19 or no longer subject to an assessment.

◆ If the CSA are unable to establish your wages, because you work is temporary or you work as a jobbing contractor, then they will impose only the IMA (between £30 and £50 per week) – you might be happy to pay this.

COURT ORDERS AND PERIODIC PAYMENT ORDERS

When you are going through the divorce or separation process there will come a point when you will consider the financial position. You will have to decide whether to have your ongoing child maintenance assessed by the CSA or whether to include it in your financial settlement with your ex-partner. This financial settlement, as well as deciding what happened to the family assets, like the home and car, is designed to make a provision to consider the ongoing support for the children (and in some cases the ex-partner).

As part of the statement of arrangements for your divorce or separation, it is possible to have your solicitor include an arrangement called periodic payments, which are in fact intended to be child maintenance payments. These periodic payments are a stated amount and payable at a stated time (normally monthly or weekly). Many divorced dads are happy to use periodic payment orders as a fair way of paying child support. The amount of money will in the first instance be a sum that is either agreed by both parties or assessed by the judge who is making out the order, the payment of which is then made over the term of that order (normally until the child is 19).

If you and your ex-partner are in agreement, then the judge is likely to ratify what your wishes are. Clearly there is great mileage in trying to mediate a settlement prior to getting in front of a judge.

◆ If your children are young, child maintenance over the long term can be a significant expense – and even more expensive can be the wrangling over how much. If possible, mediate a settlement as quickly as possible.

◆ Don't over commit. You still need to consider your own financial needs.

◆ Make sure that your ex-partner knows about all your new expenses, as it will help in your negotiations.

◆ If you have hidden money away, or have assets that your ex-partner does not know about, then keep them hidden.

◆ Plan your negotiations.

It may be that as a result of giving up equity in your home (or other assets) that your ex-partner is reasonable about child maintenance. In which case, a court order for periodic payments is generally the best deal for a divorced dad. The great thing about an order is that it means that your ex-partner cannot go along at a later date to the CSA and obtain an additional amount. Only if a judge sets the court order aside can your ex-partner seek to involve the CSA. However, your ex can go back through the legal process and obtain a variance to the original order.

The benefits of a court order

The main benefit with a court order is that it is fixed. If your income increases as a result of a pay rise or a promotion or a new job, then having a court order works in your favour, as there is no need to return to court for a new order to be made out (it is always a good idea not to let your ex-partner know about any positive changes in your financial health!).

So if you are quite young, and you think that you will progress in your career, then a court order could be the best way for you to arrange your child maintenance. Also, a court order can't deduct any money at source, so if you get bonuses or other benefits they can remain outside the payments; you don't need to tell your ex-partner about any of these additional payments that you receive (as long as you don't make the mistake of spending it in front of her).

Court orders are also not changed quickly. This is a double-edged sword and can act as both a benefit and a curse. From the positive point of view, the fact that there is a time delay in going through the legal process means that any increase in payments can be delayed, and also gives you the chance to hide any details that you can get away with. Court orders are also beneficial because their existence prevents your ex-partner from going to the CSA – which avoids a lot of stress and paperwork for any divorced dad.

The negatives of a court order

There are some negatives, and they revolve around change. If your circumstances change for the worse – you get made redundant, for example – you are still tied into the court order amount for child maintenance until you can obtain a variance – unless you can get your ex to agree to a reduction for the period of the unemployment.

That means that you will still have to continue to pay the full amount of maintenance even though your income may be non-existent. If you are going to be out of work for only a short time, then this of course will only be a minor problem and the cost of going to court for a variance will not be worth it. However, if the redundancy is for an extended period, then it could be worthwhile applying to court for a variance.

TIP

Remember that if you get a job which pays less, then the fact that a court order is fixed works against you, as payment will be fixed at the old rate.

However, the biggest negative of having a court order is apparent only when the father has to go back to court to get it changed. Many divorced dads report that judges, in order to make an accurate assessment, order an almost forensic-type investigation to their finances. Judges can, and frequently will, order divorced dads to produce (and give to their ex-partner) copies of relevant bank statements for the last twelve months, along with listings of any assets and their values that they may have.

Clearly not many divorced dads, after several years of separation, want to give that level of details to their ex-partner, but they can be ordered to do so by a judge and have no choice. The judge then makes a new order of payment based on this updated information. It is almost as if the judiciary think that divorced dads are automatically trying to get out of paying a fair level of maintenance under a court order, and therefore go over the top in ensuring that they are not hiding anything.

Clearly if you have nothing to hide then this is not a negative. But most divorced dads who carefully rebuild their assets do not wish to let their ex-partner know what their financial state is.

Changing the court order

If you or your ex-partner wants to make a change in a court order, then it is a relatively simple but slow process. By filling in the appropriate form (available from the court reception), for a nominal fee (currently about £60) you can apply to the court for a change or variance to the order. The court will set a date for a court hearing, and the legal process will grind away until both parties have presented whatever point of view they have and argued the case.

It goes without saying that mediation is better than any court action, if only to save on the legal expenses for both parties. So in the event that you need to make a change to your existing order you are better off trying to do so informally with your ex than going (in the first instance) to the court.

A major point to be considered here is that you can be liable for the costs of your ex-partner's application for maintenance payment. If a judge thinks that you have been unreasonable, and not taken sufficient steps to discuss and agree the issues with your ex-partner, or that you are just being unfair, he can award costs to either party. Solicitors' bills usually run into the thousands, so picking up the costs for both sides is not a scenario you can afford.

If you have a court order for child maintenance then you are subject to a forensic examination of your finances when an application for a change in the order is changed.

◆ This investigation is subject to a court order.

◆ The judge will ask to see copies of bank statements, and any other financial records.

◆ The judge may backdate the order, giving him details over at least a twelve-month period.

◆ Copies of all this information will need to be sent to your ex-partner's solicitor.

◆ At a court hearing you will be asked to explain every item of income, and made to justify any claims that you make on expenses.

◆ Your ex's finances may also be subject to a court order, but if she has a partner, his records will not be required.

Getting rid of a court order

As with other types of court order it cannot be discharged until the applicant (normally the divorced dad) agrees to do so. Your ex-partner cannot go to court and ask the judge to discharge the order if it has been drawn up carefully, and if you are still abiding by the terms of that order. This means that court orders can be irrevocable, and once your ex has agreed to the terms it binds both parties (subject to any variances in that order).

However, if you wish to get rid of the order then you can apply for a variance – giving the judge reasons why it is not possible for you to adhere to the term of that order – and make changes that you wish as many times as you like – or can afford!

CSA vs COURT ORDERS

Which is best? The reality of today's court system is that many judges are mindful of the guidelines which the CSA are imposing and are increasingly likely to make similar orders for amounts that the CSA would have imposed, had the case been referred to the agency. If there is no agreement between the parties prior to going to court then most judges will now make an order along the lines of the CSA rules.

So if you are one of the 97 per cent of people who are employed on a PAYE system then, it is likely that the amount you would pay under a court order is similar to what would be assessed by the CSA. Which should be a signal for all parents to make an informal arrangement in the first place – and avoid the lengthy and tedious application process!

Court orders

If you can get your ex-partner to agree to a reduced rate of child maintenance (ie lower than the CSA guidelines) – perhaps because she has kept the family house, or she earns as much or more than you do – then you are better off using a court order rather than the CSA, whose formula does not take into account settlement agreements or your ex-partner's income.

If your ex-partner is reasonable, then a court order is probably the way to go for both of you, as it can be linked to your other financial arrangements and avoids another process and a long and arduous paperwork exercise.

CSA

If you are self employed then you are probably better off going via the CSA, as you will not want to have a close examination of your finances every couple of years by a judge. Also, the ability of someone self-employed to 'hide' money will mean that any CSA assessment could be generous to you.

In addition, if your ex wants to 'bleed you dry', you are better with the CSA, as new regulations make the positions of the parties much clearer. So whether it is better for you to go via the court or the CSA depends on your personal circumstances, and your ex-partner's attitude to your finances.

Whatever the result, you will end up paying a sum of money to your ex-partner for the upkeep of your children. This is fair, and each divorced dad should shoulder his responsibility fairly and regularly. You will need to ignore the fact that you cannot influence how that money is spent and try to make the best of your own financial affairs once the arrangement has been made and ratified.

7

Ongoing parenting: becoming a great dad

YOUR NEW LIFE: GOOD AND BAD

After the first few months of the actual separation – after the upheaval when the initial problems (such as where you live and when you get to see the kids) are solved, the life of the average divorced dad falls into a new routine. This new routine is dramatically different from the one that was left behind. For most divorced dads it means:

◆ becoming the non-resident parent of his children;

◆ managing on a different budget (most often with less money to spend);

◆ interacting with his kids on a weekly, rather than daily, basis.

But for all divorced dads there are also many benefits and new opportunities. You may now have a lot more time on your hands to develop a new life. It also means that a lot of the frustrations in your relationship with your ex-partner – (which may have caused you to split up) are no longer present – and some of the stress associated with the old marital life is dissipated.

Many divorced dads achieve a freedom from daily routines that enables them to go on to develop a new life. Of course this new balance also has its drawbacks. For many divorced dads, seeing the children less is a major concern; being less of an influence in their lives than when living at home is a situation which many fathers feel bad about. But over time the emotions associated with this new position calm down, and you can get on with the job of being a dad under the circumstances that you are now in.

Getting on with the ex

There are many factors that determine the success of the your ongoing parenting. Your children's needs, and your ability to provide for those needs, are of course key elements. But possibly the biggest factor is your relationship with your ex-partner.

TIP
Parenting is about teamwork, and is done well if all the members of the team know what the team's strategy is – and act as a team to achieve the best result.

To use a football analogy – the defence and the attack need to work together towards the same goal.

What many divorced dads find is that the relationship that they have with their ex-partner changes dramatically over time. During the separation the relationship is at its most strained – even if the break up is a mutual decision. (For some people this unfortunately goes as far as open warfare, with acts of revenge from both parties.)

But generally after the first few months drift into a year or two years, and mum and dad have started to establish new lives for themselves, a relationship of convenience is established between them. The parents develop a level of co-operation which enables them to act as a team. Although they may not be in the premiership, but probably performing somewhere down in the conference, a state evolves that enables both parents to operate. Generally, as time goes by and the kids get older and more able to control their own affairs, the parents find a way of operating around each other.

Coping with a new life

Dealing with the initial separation is only the first hurdle that you have to overcome if you are to become the great dad that you always wanted to be. Some pieces of your new life will make that goal easier to achieve – you establish a new home, and some new hobbies with your children for example. Some barriers, such as your ex's attitude will be removed – probably slowly.

Situations will arise that put your relationship with your children at risk: changes in your own life such as new relationships, or new jobs, for example, are things which can have a dramatic effect on your current relationship with your children.

You will face an ever-changing environment, and will need to cope with any changes that arise, and strive to continue to make the best of the situation for the benefit of your kids. It will not be an easy ride – and for many divorced dads situations arise that test them to the limit and beyond.

SO YOU STILL WANT TO BE A GREAT DAD?

During the first phase of separation and divorce, many elements of a father's life are in a process of change – where he lives, what he does with his time, his financial position, and so on. This period of time normally ranges from two to 12 months, depending on the circumstances of the separation. But you will reach a stage where the emotional, physical and financial disturbance is over and it is time to think about where to go from here and what the balance in your life is going to be.

Working out a balance

Being divorced does not mean that your desire to be the greatest possible dad to your children changes; nor does it alter the fact that you are that one special person in their lives. Even though circumstances have changed, it does not mean that you have to change the expectations of the role that you will play in their lives, but you will have to alter how you achieve your goal.

One of the most important considerations in reaching this goal is to work out what your long-term parenting plan is going to be. Some of this will be determined already, but much of it is in your hands. Although you can still achieve a lot if you take a casual approach to how your relationship with your children will develop, it is better to put a little planning into it: they say that 'proper planning leads to perfect results'.

THE IMPORTANCE OF NEVER LOSING CONTACT

For a moment, put yourself in your children's shoes if you can. Try and see the world from their perspective. A child has very few anchor points in their lives: school, pets, a home, and most importantly their mum and dad. When there is separation or divorce, a major anchor in their life becomes loose. And they don't quite realise why. In some separations several anchors can go at the same time, if the mum also has to move home, or the child is separated from their pet for example.

Every child needs as stable an upbringing as their parents can possibly give them. Providing an environment of security and love is possibly the most important responsibility that parents share. A major part of that security and love comes from having the father around.

Always remember that just because you and your partner get divorced, your children don't choose to lose a parent; no child ever would. Depending on the circumstances of the separation, and the age/development of the child, there may be a temporary phase of alienation as the child does not understand the true reasons for the changes in their lives. They may say things like, 'I don't ever want to see you again', but this is because of confused loyalties and heightened emotions. They may position themselves on the side of one of the parents, but you need to recognise this for what it really is, and not read more in to it than the child trying to make both parents listen to what they need.

TIP
It is your responsibility to make every effort to remain in your child's life, and that responsibility rests with you alone.

It may be very difficult to carry out, with obstructions placed in your way, and future changes in your life, but even though contact with your child will change and vary over the childhood, it is critical that you remain in contact in some form. This may well be the biggest challenge that you have to face.

Never lose contact with your children. If you have to move away because of work or other pressures, always leave an avenue of contact, no matter how small.

The effect of losing contact

If you are the type of father who is not going to be a positive influence on your children's lives, then I doubt very much you are reading this book. The role of dad probably means very little to these fathers – perhaps because of the role that their dads had in their lives. Whatever the reason, there are at least two people who will suffer as a result of that decision: the child and the dad.

There are many stories of people who were abandoned by a parent when young, from celebrities such as Mick Hucknall (lead singer of Simply Red), to normal people with normal jobs and lives, but no matter who it is it is very difficult for relationships to be re-established once contact is broken. Each story has its own set of circumstances, and we cannot judge the right or wrong of them. But both child and parent suffers instead of benefiting from having each other in their lives.

The effect on the child

Most importantly, the child misses having the father as a positive influence in their lives. They miss having their real dad to talk to, and to love, because it is in the nature of all children to love without judgement. If you fail to keep in contact with your children they will miss out on being able to love you.

But this is not only the way the child misses out, as dads have an important role to play in a child's development. All children need encouragement and guidance as well as confidence. The appropriate words at the right time during the endeavours of childhood can create a confidence that will enable the child to keep on trying, to achieve more and to get fulfilment from school, play and home.

TIP

You don't need to be a child psychologist to be a good dad; you simply need to be around to provide guidance, encouragement and words of wisdom as your children experience new things.

If you fail to keep in contact then you will be failing to have a positive influence in inspiring your child to achieve to the best of their abilities.

The effect on the dad

But it is not only the child that misses out if you lose contact. Most dads find that the experience of being a father is a very rewarding and enjoyable one and cannot be surpassed by other activities or roles in their lives. In fact this is a double-edged sword, as the effect of a divorce is to limit how much influence you can have, which seems to heighten awareness of what you're missing.

If you fail to keep up contact with your children, you will miss out on an opportunity to achieve fulfilment in your life. It is logical to say that the bigger the role you play in your child's life, the greater the fulfilment both you and your child will achieve. You have satisfaction in your own life, and become more contented as you grow and develop as a person.

If you choose not to stay in contact with your children you lose the right to have a positive influence on their upbringing. You also lose the right to walk back into your child's life when they are an adult; they should have the right to decide if they would like anything to do with you.

Also, because a child needs a dad, your ex-partner may well get your child to call another man dad; if you are still in contact with your children this is wrong but if you have fled the scene it may in fact be good and help to give them a balanced upbringing. In short – if you leave your child's life, then you also leave behind an opportunity to find fulfilment yourself, and will surely damage the emotional upbringing of your child.

As a child grows

You can't predict the future, or what your child's needs will be in the later years of their childhood. It may be that the relationship with the resident parent will deteriorate and they will need a bolt hole to flee to. Adolescence and puberty create a lot of strains at home, and having a dad round the corner to turn to can be a godsend to a child who is having problems at home. If you are there for them your relationship will continue to grow. But the lack of a dad to go to can leave a child with nowhere to turn. In the worst case this can lead to leaving home too young – perhaps even living on the street and getting into trouble. Of course, this is a worst-case scenario, but do remember what you can offer your child by staying in touch.

Also, whilst contact can be obstructed at the early stages of a divorce, as the child gets older they will want to have a bigger influence over contact arrangements, and will determine more for themselves what contact they want. At that stage, the obstructions that your ex may have put in the way of your contact will almost certainly disappear. If you have maintained a relationship until that point then your relationship with your child will develop very quickly and without the constraints of the past, enabling both of you to really benefit from each other.

LONG-TERM PARENTING PLAN

So you have made the decision to support your children as they grow up and to be a positive influence in their lives. Now you have to consider how to be a great dad in the future.

Your relationship with your child is a result of the time and energy that you spend with them. The purpose of a long-term plan is to ensure that you have a balanced relationship which caters for the needs of your children, as well as your own needs. Clearly, dealing with children of different ages will involve different criteria. If your child is preschool, their needs will be different to a teenager. But at whatever level or age your child is, try to communicate with them and let them know what to expect.

Most divorced dads don't consider a long-term plan, but the process does have significant benefits. You don't have to have a plan straight way – it can evolve.

◆ A plan can clarify your thinking and consolidate ideas, or help you realise that you are not doing enough.

- It can help to talk to other divorced dads to get some ideas.

- Think about what shared interests you can develop with your children.

- Don't be afraid to realise that there are things that you cannot achieve.

- Don't be overly ambitious; you can always expand it later.

Making a plan involves a great deal of thinking; you will need to think about future changes, and not make promises that you cannot keep in the future. The more that you think about how best to achieve your goal of being a great dad the better you will probably turn out.

Remember that you are one of a few hundred thousand divorced dads in the UK, who are all going through the same process as you. If you can talk to some of them to find out what they have done to make things work, it is a good place to start in putting together your long-term parenting plan.

You need to consider the following areas:

- **Money:** what you need to pay for.

- **Home:** where the children will live and how you will create a second home for them.

- **School:** what involvement you want at school.

- **Family:** how you want other members of your family to be involved.

- **New family:** how you will deal with their step dad, or your new partner.

- **Holidays:** what you can do.

- **Religion:** if you have any beliefs that you want them to follow.

In addition to these you need to think about your own life:

- **Balancing** your life with the needs of the kids.

- **Your home** – what it needs to be.

- **Communicating** with your ex-partner: how you are going to do it, especially if there is friction.

- **Joint issues** – you will need to agree with your ex-partner on issues affecting your children such as smoking, drinking, staying up late and so on.

The benefit of a parenting plan

For some divorced dads there is very little benefit as they are very much isolated in their role, and don't have any influence with their ex-partner on how the children should be brought up. But any responsible dad should at least try to agree with his ex some shared principles on the upbringing of their kids. It's important to try to be on the same team.

Some divorced dads who have limited contact find that their role in the children's daily life is superficial, but that does not mean to say that they have to totally abdicate their responsibility to be a positive influence. Even Sunday dads can, in the time that they have, uphold views that they want their child to absorb as they grow older.

A Sunday dad can at least do the following:

◆ Eat a good meal on the day rather than having fast food – promoting healthy eating.

◆ Do some form of sport – promoting exercise.

◆ Discuss the importance of qualifications – promoting academic success.

◆ Take an interest in the activities of the child – encouraging endeavour.

◆ Show love – always what every child needs.

Communicating with your ex

If you have a greater influence in your children's lives, it is critical to develop a plan for their future that you and your ex-partner agree on. Work out when, where and how often you are going to discuss matters, and when communicating with her, think about the following:

◆ Respect her view if she offers a different one.

◆ Support her as a parent – and that support will come back to you.

◆ Think about the continuing needs of the child – not about how it was in the past.

◆ Remember that mistakes will be made – be prepared to be flexible.

The more you can get your ex-partner to agree to, the less of a struggle you will have in getting the time with your children. For example, if your ex-partner agrees to let you take your children to swimming lessons – because the children need to learn to swim – then you will automatically get the time with your children. You can then build on this, especially if it means no work or inconvenience for your ex, who quite naturally will justify to herself letting you take them swimming because the kids benefit.

TIP

The more that your ex-partner thinks you are acting in conjunction with her feelings and thoughts the better the relationship with her will be. That is one of the keys to having a long-term impact on your kids' lives.

CASE STUDY

Working with mum
Dad: Alan
Children: Kyle (age 16), Imogen (age 13)
Situation: Separated for two years

Two years ago my ex-partner and I decided that it was time to split up. Our relationship was not improving, and in order to avoid further disputes we decided to live apart. As it happens we have not yet got around to getting divorced. I know that we will one day – it is not as if we will ever get back together – but at the moment we are working together.

The kids took it better than we expected. There were tears and lots of hugs the day we sat them down and told them, and it is a day that I won't forget. But the fact that they were both in secondary school helped a lot because they were used to their friends' parents being divorced so they knew that it was not the end of the world. And also because they were that bit older and more mature – they could understand things a lot better.

My ex has always been a career woman, and I have my own business, so I can be flexible around times that I see the kids. This has really helped, because I see them every day. I pick my daughter up from school, and help her to get to gymnastics classes as well as her other activities, and my son knows he can rely on me to be a bit of a taxi.

My ex-partner and I don't agree on everything – I guess that is why we agreed to a separation. There are times when the kids are in conflict with their mum. When this happens I don't always back her, but I do ask the kids to respect the fact that they live under her roof. Because of these conflicts they are both asking to come and live with me, but I have persuaded them to go back home, knowing that a bit of time will see them all calm down. Deep down I know that they are better off living with her and seeing me every day.

Being separated does not mean that I miss out on the kids because I take the same role as I did when I was married – supporting them in their activities. I have a standard routine with both my son and daughter, which means that I get to pick them up from school and take them to whatever activity they are going to – or just bring them to my house for tea, until their mum returns from work. I know that she still needs me to look after the kids after school because of her work commitments, and I think that this helps to keep things on an even keel, and keeps her amicable.

What I love about being separated is that I can be the type of dad that I want to be. I am a bit more relaxed about the kids than their mum is. I will allow them to grow up, whereas I feel that she is over protective. I let the kids grow up and stretch their wings more, which I wouldn't be able to do if I was still married. I really think that this has helped me to build my relationship with the children as they become teenagers.

So my life is great now. I have my own space, I have my kids and my freedom, and all without any conflict with my ex. The key to it is being reasonable with each other and communicating – we still talk about the contact arrangements, about ongoing issues, and about things that the kids do. Even though the kids communicate with me directly I still keep a channel open with my ex. And as parents we try to operate as a team.

Communicating with your children

How and when best to communicate with your children is also a part of your long-term plan. Other divorced dads have found it very useful to establish at the earliest opportunity an independent method of communicating with the children, whether by email, or by buying a mobile phone (even if it only has a text message package). This clearly cannot be done when they are five or six, but as soon as they reach nine or ten, then you can establish a communications channel.

Try to do this in agreement with your ex-partner, and make it a special event for your kids. You could, for example buy the phone as a birthday present. But don't force your child to use it; don't make them feel as if they *have* to phone or email you. It is better for you to be casual about this, or you will make them feel as if communicating with you is a chore.

Living arrangements

When thinking about long-term living arrangements for you and the children, you need to understand that children view their home as one of the primary anchor points in their lives. For a child a home means stability, and the more stability there is in your child's upbringing the better. This is why conflict at home is such a terrible influence in a child's life because it undermines one of the bedrocks of a child's existence.

In the majority of situations, children spend most of the time living with mum. They visit their dad's home and stay there overnight, or for the weekend.

TIP

It is important to create a space in your new home for your children; somewhere they can keep their toys, clothes, and a space that they can play in.

If you can achieve this – creating a second home for your children – then they will have another anchor point, and their stability will be improved.

It may be that in the initial stage of your separation you are not able to create a second home for your children, but this is something that you can do after things have settled down. When you do get the opportunity, it is important that you allow your child to personalise it as much as possible; let them put their own character and personality into it. If you can, let them decorate their room or put posters up (they may even be able to decorate it in a way they're not allowed at their mum's house). This is a good way of creating a feeling that they own the place, or have some stake in your new home. And getting them to help in the redecoration of the room can be lots of fun!

The DfCA study shows that overnight stays do not happen as often as they could or should – with almost 20 per cent of children not having overnight stays with dad, and fewer than 35 per cent of children having overnight stays more than once a week.

Overnight stays are critical in developing your relationship with your children, as you get to share in their weekly routines, and establish some new ones in your house. Children also benefit from overnight stays as it makes them feel part of your life. And, as mentioned before, the creation of a second home gives them another anchor in their lives, another area of stability to build on.

The report says:

A third (33%) of children in the non-resident parent sample stay overnight with their non-resident parent at least once a week.

The message is clear – if you can, be one of the 33 per cent of fathers who have their children for overnight stays during the week. This is especially important if the children are under ten years old. You can create some really special memories.

Being involved with school

School is an area where you must get involved. As part of your long-term plan, you need to take an active interest in your children's school lives. This is because school is such a big part of their life; it is where they gain most friends, where they pick up all sorts of influences and information (good and bad) and where they spend every week day.

It may be that your kid is not particularly academic, or interested in school, but you still need to encourage them to be as good a pupil as they can, to work hard and to behave themselves. School is not only where your children learn academic matters but where they also learn a lot of other stuff about life. It is a place where they form friendships, and a place where they are subject to the views of their peers. It is true that kids can be cruel to one another – and if your child is suffering at school, then you need to know and understand if you are to advise them how to handle the pressures of school life.

◆ Always discuss school with your children.

◆ Take an active interest in their achievements.

◆ Make sure that the school is sending you information on what is going on.

◆ Make sure that you attend parents evenings.

◆ Consider becoming a school governor.

◆ Consider becoming a classroom assistant (if you can spare the time).

◆ Perhaps give some rewards for good behaviour or for success at exams.

◆ Encourage your kids to go on school trips (even if you have to make the money available).

◆ Encourage your kids to take part in after school clubs (again, even if you have to pay).

◆ Get to know you children's school friends by inviting them to join you on your activities with your children.

Medical issues

Your child's health is always important; it may even be that your child suffers from a medical condition. Make sure that as part of your plan you have considered the following:

◆ What, if any, your children's special needs are.

◆ What to do if your child becomes ill during your contact.

◆ How you will be kept updated on your child's health.

You may need to have a discussion with your ex-partner about your child's health issues, and agree a plan if your child suffers an accident or gets an illness. It is always best to agree this prior to the event as the stress of dealing with the accident at the time may mean that your ex-partner does not think clearly or doesn't know whether to contact you or not. It is best to decide this early on so that whatever is agreed between the parents can simply just happen.

Teenagers

If your children are of an age where they want a say in their upbringing and their relationship with you, it is natural to involve them in this process. You can sit down with your young adult and have an open discussion with them about where and how you want them to be a part of your life. Give them the opportunity to tell you where they feel they would benefit from having you around (and of course discuss how much cash you are going to give them for their allowance!). Taking this approach with young adults is necessary, as if you involve them in the discussion they are more likely to adhere to the agreements. You will probably get a huge buzz out of doing this; certainly your teenager will, as they seek to take more responsibility for their own lives and time, and to be treated as an adult.

Where possible, involve your children in the design of your long-term parenting plan.

◆ Talk to other parents who have kids of a similar age and discover what their interaction with their teenagers is.

◆ Be prepared for some unusual requests.

◆ Be flexible: your ideas may not be shared by your teenagers.

◆ Be prepared to express your own desires, but allow your teenager to express theirs.

◆ If you don't have agreement, then don't expect it to work!

◆ Don't expect to get it right first time – you will need to evolve the plan.

◆ If it works, don't change it.

◆ If it is broken, look for a solution with all the parties involved.

◆ Be prepared to be let down – if your teenager wants to go to a party instead of seeing you then you might have to face being second choice.

Without a shadow of a doubt, communication is vital to achieve an active part in a teenager's life. It means that they participate in the things that you plan to a greater extent, and your relationship with them flourishes rather than flounders. Many divorced dads realise that because they are not a part of their teenager's daily struggle, they can become a great friend to them at this time. If they rebel, they rebel against their mum. For many divorced dads, being divorced from the teenager's mum mean that they can develop a better relationship with their children than if they still lived at the family home.

Younger children

Unfortunately many divorced dads don't get to spend that many years at the family home, and their children are still under five when their relationship with the ex-partner breaks down. So the evolution of their parenting goals is a little more complicated and probably subject to many more restraints. These restraints come primarily in the form of the contact/access times that are agreed (whether through a court order or voluntarily) with your ex-partner. Other restraints may also exist: accommodation, finances, another partner, geographic distance for example.

Distance

Geographic distance between dad and his children can be a major problem. Evidence from the DfCA report shows that if a divorced dad moves away from his children he is less likely to have direct or indirect contact with them. (Direct contact meaning actually seeing the kids and indirect contact meaning things such as phone contact.)

Results show that distance between the homes of the child and their non-resident parent have a significant impact upon the frequency of contact between the child and their non-resident parent. Children who lived less than ten miles from their non-resident parent were more likely to have direct contact at least once a week than children who lived further away. Similarly, children who lived fifty miles or more from their non-resident parent were those most likely to have no contact with their non-resident parent.

Contact less frequently than once a week would also appear to be affected by the distance between the child and their non-resident parent . . . Children who lived between 10 and 49 miles from their non-resident parent were three times as likely to have direct contact less often than once a week than direct contact once a week compared with children who lived within 10 miles of their non-resident parents. The odds of having direct contact less often than once a week than having direct contact at least once week was 23 times more likely for children who lived 50 miles or more from their non-resident parent than those who lived less than ten miles.

It may be a crucial part of any father's long-term parenting plan to remain local to his children. This could even mean sacrificing a part of his career, or it could hamper any future relationships. The message from the study is clear: if a father moves away, then it is likely that he will lose some form of either direct or indirect contact with his children.

Developing shared interests

Whatever the age of your children, or the extent of your contact, you will enjoy a better relationship with your child if you can develop shared interests. Your role as a divorced dad is no different in this respect from when you were at home; one of inspiring your child and helping them broaden their horizons to develop an active and fulfilling life.

If you were the type of father that was happy to allow your child to sit in front of a computer game for the day, now is the time to change. Your child can do that at home, without you. Not only is it a failure on your part to develop your child, it is not physically healthy over the long term. In today's society there is an increasing trend for children to have weight problems, and to become obese. You don't want to add to the problem by encouraging your kids to be sedentary in their lifestyle. You want them to become healthy and develop physically.

TIP

Your idea of a great time may be different to your child's. At the time you have access, your children's desires come first!

Finding balance
The only way to add any value to your child's life is by throwing some energy at it. That is not to say that you should exclude all computer games – it's fine for them to beat dad at the latest Grand Prix racing game, or kill more aliens than you! For some of the time at least. Life is about balance – and you need to design your time and activities with the children in a balanced way.

Finding activities
Shared interests are exactly what they say: both you and your children need to enjoy them. This is easy to manage when you have just one child, but developing a programme of shared interests for girls and boys of different ages can sometimes be a challenge. Especially if you only have access to your children all at the same time.

Work on finding something to share. It may be something where you are only a spectator, or you might be there alongside them taking part. Whatever your involvement, your role is to encourage, support and inspire.

Shared activities do not have to cost money. Your children will benefit from the energy that you put into them, not how much they cost. Simple activities such as walking in the country, swimming and cycling can be done by all ages together.

Don't expect your children to want to support you in your activities. Just because you have an interest doesn't mean that they will want to do it as well. Spending the day on the banks of the river fishing may be a great way for you to relax, but might not be what your children want to do. You might be a Manchester United fan, but they might prefer to spend the day watching cricket! You have to communicate with them and find out what is best for you both to develop as a shared interest.

If at your times of access you would normally watch your local football team, but your children have no interest, forcing them to spend a cold day sat on the terraces will not create the bond that you want. Miss the match that week, or engineer your contact times around any existing activities that you have so that you don't miss out, so your child doesn't have to participate in activities which they find boring.

However, many children are heavily influenced by the existing activities of their parents. Why else would Tim Henman have become a tennis player, or Angelina Jolie an actress? So if your child shows some enjoyment in doing the same things as you, then you are on to a winner. It makes access and activities so much easier if you can develop your interests together.

If you have a passion for a hobby, then that enthusiasm will be transferred (as if by magic) to the child, as children enjoy both the activity itself and also enjoy seeing their dad get a lot of fun out of doing it as well. Remember, children will be more relaxed and prepared to enjoy themselves if they see you are doing so as well.

Most divorced dads can get quite exhausted looking after their children for the access periods, and it is even more pronounced if they are doing it on their own. By absorbing yourself and your children in shared activities the time will fly by to the extent that spending energy on your children takes very little effort indeed.

A SUBSTITUTE DAD

It is probable that at some point in the future (if it has not happened already) your ex-partner will find someone new, and he will move in and have a relationship not only with her, but also with your children. It may be that this new man has children of his own to add to the household, or indeed is himself a divorced dad. The relationship that you will have with this man can range from a mutual respect and understanding, to aggression and profound hatred.

Naturally you will be concerned as to the impact that this man will have, and you will ask yourself a whole range of questions:

- Is he a paedophile?
- Does he deal in drugs?
- Is he from a weird religion?
- Does he support the right football team?

It is quite normal to have some concerns as to whether this man will be good for your children, and what your children will think of him. What will his attitude to you be? And what about your attitude to him? What will the kids call him? Many questions are raised when another adult starts to spend time with your children.

His background

Under UK law, you do not have the right to find out whether another individual has a criminal record. As a result of recent child murders there have been many calls to open up the records of known paedophiles so that the public would know who they were, and if their children were at risk. Children are in danger and the public still can't find out what they are facing in their communities; you have no chance of accessing any official information about a man who moves in with your kids.

So whatever your concerns, you have no way of finding out what kind of bloke he is, other than talking to him, or to others who know him. Unless you have loads of money, in which case you can always get a private detective to run a report for you!

If your relationship with your ex-partner is OK, then clearly you can talk to her. But be aware that you are likely to get a rose-tinted picture of him.

His attitude to you

There are at least three factors that will heavily influence this. Firstly, the picture your ex-partner has painted about you, as he will have discussed you in depth with your ex prior to having any contact. Secondly, how aware he is of his role and responsibilities to your children, and thirdly whether he has had any experience of this type of situation before.

If your ex-partner has painted a picture that you are a reasonable man, then he will be open to discussion. However, if her description of you is somewhat closer to Attila the Hun then you can expect that to influence his perception of you pretty negatively.

This new bloke's position with your ex-partner has given him new responsibilities, which he may handle poorly, or with great skill. What you need to realise is that this new man may not be intelligent enough to realise what his actions should be, and what long-term impact they will have on your kids. If he is bit dense then one thing is for sure, if you have already been aligned with Attila the Hun, he is not going to take advice from you.

If he has been there before – has already had a relationship with another woman who had kids at home – this will influence his judgement, and his prior experiences will affect his actions. He will inadvertently bring some emotional baggage from his previous encounters with him.

The least that you should expect from him as far as his attitude to you is that he:

◆ respects your relationship with your children;

◆ respects your role in your children's life;

◆ does not seek to take over your position as dad to your children.

These three things are the subjects that you need to discuss with him and your ex-partner.

Your attitude to him

Your attitude to him may be clouded by your attitude to your ex. If you hate her for kicking you out of the home, forcing you to spend only a little time with the kids, and grabbing every penny that you have, then another bloke spending time and having an influence on your kids may send you into a seething rage.

Especially if this is within a couple of weeks – or less – of the separation. Your anger is real. But if you direct it at this new bloke for no reason then you are acting irrationally; you must at least give the bloke a chance at the start.

You may feel a great deal of emotional pain if you think that this man is spending more time than you with your children. You may even resent him because he represents the lack of control you now have over your children's lives. But you have to respect the right that he has to have a relationship with your ex-partner (as long as he does not harm your kids). He will also, because he is there, have a relationship with your kids.

There is nothing that you need be afraid of, because you have the power to deal with this situation – mental strength, not brute force. You also have your children on your side. They don't forget who their real parents are, and their loyalty (providing it is not abused) is always there, so you don't need to worry that you will be replaced in the long-term. From their perspective, you will always be their real dad.

What will the children call him?

Probably the biggest sin that your ex-partner can commit is encouraging your children to call another man dad. They do it, against your wishes, when they are still in conflict with you. It is their attempt to undermine the strong relationship that you have with your children; it can be done out of pure spite and malice and with no regard to the needs of your child.

It can also be done simply because your ex-partner wants to make the new bloke feel more comfortable about spending time and energy with your kids. Again, this is normally motivated by your ex's need to comfort her new man, rather than driven by the needs of the child.

If you have an active and positive relationship with your kids then your ex-partner has no right to try to usurp your position, by substituting you with another dad. But that won't stop her doing so.

There are other terms, such as 'biological parent' and 'real dad', which are trendy but not necessarily helpful. If you only ever wanted to be a biological parent, then you should be happy to take that title. But if, as in the vast majority of cases, you became a dad because you wanted to be a great parent and raise your children, and providing you have stuck to that task to the best of your ability, then you have the moral right to be the only man in that child's life with the title of dad.

TIP

Bear in mind that if your new partner has children and you have a relationship with them the same applies to you; you need to respect the position of the real dad.

The best way for your children to address your ex-partner's new man is quite simply by his first name. You will find that if he understands his responsibilities in his relationship with your child, and he fully respects your position, then he will have no issues with this. However, if he does not understand them well, then he will take a different course. Here you are snookered, because clearly you have no control over how intelligent or aware the new bloke actually is, and if he does not respect your position then the last person on earth he will take any advice from is you.

Your children's attitude to him

Again, there are several things that will influence this and it is very much age related. Younger children, naturally, seek to please their mum and any adults around them, whilst older children may resent him for replacing you. Secretly they may still want you and your ex to get back together so will be hostile to the new partner. If they are teenagers, their attitude may well be, 'You're not my dad so stop telling me to be quiet in *my* house. Why don't you just p*** off?'

Another factor which will influence their attitude is timing. If the new partner turns up at the door just as you have left, then older children are far more likely to be hostile than if they have had time to get used to the fact that you are not there. Younger children are likely to be confused about the role of the new partner, and unfortunately it is difficult to explain to a five year old what is really going on.

You may want to agree with your child's hostile feelings, but however strong the inclination is, you should avoid it.

This is the time where you need to take the moral high ground – it is always best to promote good relations between your children and new partners, but if you feel unable to do this, then at least don't promote hostility. That would be like teaching them that is OK to fight, to rebel, which may come back to haunt you one day. It is better to teach them to be nice than horrible.

Saying something like, 'I know you don't like him, and I'm not sure myself, but it is your mother's choice not yours or mine to make. Anyway you can always move out in a few years' time if you don't like it,' doesn't help. It may also plant an idea in the child's mind that might be difficult for you to live up to.

Dealing with the new man

The best possible position is one where the adults all respect each other's relationships, are aware of everyone's needs, and think of the children's needs before their own. That would be a perfect world! But we don't live in utopia, nor do we live in a world where people respect everyone else's rights. John Lennon sang about that in his song 'Imagine', but even though he was a divorced dad, he did not have to deal with *your* ex-partner!

So what can you do?

Your emotional state at this stage might be very fragile, and the last thing that you want to do is to have an adult conversation with a bloke that does not respect you, especially now that he has usurped your position in your old house. It's not a nice fact but you just have to face it. You have to remember that you are now separated, and it is the future that is of primary importance.

You are expected to interact with this person normally, and whilst this might be the last thing on earth that you want to do, you *must* manage this. It is likely to be a monumental task, maybe even a tortuous process. But if you can pull it off your children will benefit, and so will you.

If you act in an aggressive or argumentative manner then the reaction of your ex-partner will be to shut you out. This may affect the access you get to your children. Remember that your ex wants her new man to settle in as quietly as possible – so perhaps you can use this to your advantage, as a negotiating point with her.

CASE STUDY

Dealing with a stepdad

Dad: Joe

Child: Dan

Situation: Married for five years, divorced for six years

We separated six years ago, when my son was four. Fairly shortly afterwards my ex-wife started another relationship. My relationship with my son was well established – we got on great. So even though there were times when my ex played up a bit and got in the way of contact, it never really lasted for long and for the most part I have been able to see Dan as much as I could. Dan is now 10 years old, and comes around to see me every weekend – we do a lot together.

But my ex and I have not agreed on everything. Despite me clearly telling her my views against it, she has encouraged Dan to call her partner dad. This means that Dan now calls two people dad, and has often got confused when talking to his friends about things. My ex justifies her actions by saying that when Dan was five he wanted to call her partner dad. Well at the time I was incensed, and still am. I have always been around for Dan, and feel that my ex is simply trying to play happy families with her new partner and does not give a damn about my feelings on this subject. Unfortunately for me her new partner is dominated by her, and does not have any children of his own, so I guess he quite likes the feeling of a child calling him dad.

For my ex to justify her action by saying that a five year old wants to call him dad is pathetic. If Dan said he did not want to go to school then clearly, as adults, we would talk to him and get him to act accordingly. Part of being a good parent is knowing what is good and bad for your children.

But in this case what I and my ex believe are two different things. Unfortunately for me her desire to play happy families at home, and to make her new partner feel part of Dan's life, has more impact than the feelings or thoughts of her ex-husband. I guess I should not be surprised (after all we are divorced!), it is just that I feel that Dan would be best served by having all three adults in his life but not mistaking who is who. I asked my ex to get Dan to call her new partner by his first name, but she refused.

It does really get me down that my only son calls another man dad. None of my family or friends think that I am being unreasonable – only my ex and her new partner. I am also concerned that Dan will suffer some additional emotional damage. I could understand it if I was an absent father but I have always been his dad, and will always be around.

There is no need for Dan to be confused about what a dad is – especially as he may one day be a father himself. I want him growing up thinking that this role is special and that being a dad comes with a responsibility to his children. I don't want him growing up thinking that anybody who enters a child's life is a father. I know social attitudes are always changing, but I still believe that some of the established role models are best for children; I believe that Dan will only grow up understanding what a dad does if he is not confused about who that person is and what role they play.

I guess that when he is older I might be able to talk to him about it, to truly explain my feelings and why I believe that he should call his stepdad by his first name. Then he can decided for himself what is right and wrong – he can make his own mind up.

Talking is better than fighting

◆ Start off by trying to have open discussions with all parties.

◆ Express yourself calmly and positively.

◆ Try not to personalise your dealings with him.

◆ Understand that he has a role to play.

◆ Know that you can't control what he does, only influence it.

◆ Find out if he is already a dad; it will influence his behaviour heavily.

◆ Talk about what you don't want, and make clear any points you don't wish to talk about.

◆ Stick to only talking about your children. Don't talk about your old relationship with your ex.

◆ Don't expect him to be perfect or to agree to everything that you want.

◆ Remember that it may take several meetings to persuade him to agree to some things you want.

If talks break down

◆ Put it in writing; highlight anything that you specifically do or don't want.

◆ Don't give your kids a full breakdown of what an idiot you really think he is.

DEALING WITH STEPCHILDREN

It may well happen that you if you find a new partner she has children. What will your attitude be to them and their dad? And what will the reaction of your children be? What should the interaction between them all be?

TIP
Treat the stepchild's dad as you would want to be treated. And remember to allow all the children time to adjust to changing family relationships.

If you inherit any children with your new relationship, then obviously that brings some responsibilities as you will have a role to play in their lives. Think carefully about what your position and role should be, remembering always to put the long-term needs of the children first, and avoid potential conflict areas. If you have experienced another man failing to do this, don't replicate that behaviour.

It is always best to talk to your new partner and decide what to do in conjunction with her feelings. If the child's real dad is still taking an active part in their development, then together as a team (remembering that he has the right to be the team captain), you can really add something to the child's life. If he is not around, then the child may want you to take a bigger part in their lives and want to call you dad. There is nothing wrong with this, providing that it does not cause any conflict with any existing relationships, and of course that you intend to stay for the long term.

Talking to the dad is the key to overcoming any barriers in that area (remember that he is probably a decent bloke and not as much of a nightmare as your new partner may make out!). Just pick up the phone and tell him that you would like to know if he has any specific issues that he would like to discuss, and that you are open to hearing any comments about the children that he would like to make. If he strays onto talking about his ex-partner, calmly put him back on track. Hopefully he will be communicative. You may need to try a few times to get talking to him, as he may himself take a little time to realise what the situation is. If not, then leave the door open for him.

TIP

It may take years for stepchildren to trust and respect you.

Often their attitude to you is not based on fact or truth, but on insecurities within the child's mind. You can try talking to them, but in many cases, they themselves will not understand the psychology of what is going on in their heads.

One big thing that can help is if you are supportive of them developing close relationships with their father and other relatives. If you let them know that you are comfortable with this, then the children are more likely to feel comfortable with you.

One of the biggest problem areas with stepchildren is the disciplinary code that is practised in the household. It is likely that you and your new partner will have different ideas of how to discipline the children. This will need to be discussed with your new partner and a common approach taken. You can't have two practices, one for your kids and one for the stepchildren if they are living in the same household. It will lead to lasting resentment not only between them but also towards you. You need to sort this out with your new partner, but make sure you do it away from the kids.

TIME

Anyone who has grieved, maybe after the loss of a relative or friend, will know that time helps. Time helps to overcome raw emotions. Time helps people to move on with their lives. Time helps people come to terms with feelings of loss, and of losing a loved one. In separation even the most vociferous of couples can, with time, learn to live around each other for the benefit of the children.

Sure – there are some divorced dads who never recover from a separation, and the actual events of the separation leave such an emotional scar that it is impossible for them to be on friendly terms with the ex-partner. Some divorced dads find that this also goes on to affect their attitude towards new partners, and they are never able to trust another woman again.

But, irrespective of what happens during the process of the separation (or whatever the reason for the separation in the first place), you *must* over a period of time be able to have some form of relationship with your ex-partner – even if (as in most cases) it is a neutral or ambivalent one. The reason is clear – in order to have an unencumbered relationship with your children you need to be able to work along side your ex.

Many parents who separate manage to come to an informal arrangement for the kids. This is a 'managed position', where they work with each other for the benefit of the children. For others the situation takes longer to get to. But time can help all parents get to that position.

CASE STUDY

The effect of time
Dad: Ken
Children: Rebecca (aged seven when got divorced), Jon (five),
Adam (three)
Situation: Married for over nine years, divorced for 15 years

I have been divorced now for over 15 years, so I have lived through many of the issues of being a parent even though I am a divorced dad, and many are just the same. Whether it be having the money to pay for holidays or dealing with teenage hormones, being a dad is still being a dad even if you are not living with their mum.

Having three kids is not always an easy thing to cope with especially when they were younger. Because I worked away during the week a lot (as a truck driver) the time I would get to see them was at the weekend – and of course I would get to see them all at the same time. This was a bit of a problem as they were different ages and therefore wanted to do different activities. What Adam wanted to do when he was three was not much interest to Rebecca who was seven.

I would have the kids most weekends, though not for the night as my accommodation was not big enough, and each week the kids would take turns in deciding what they wanted to do. I let them make suggestions and come up with ideas. Clearly I was constrained by money, but for the most part they just wanted to spend time with me and do simple activities. Rebecca, the oldest, was great – she was very understanding and helped me a lot with looking after the others. The bond that developed between us during this time was fantastic. Somehow she knew most of the practical difficulties that I had, and was able to help me in all sorts of ways including communicating with her brothers.

The kids have now grown up and I have a great relationship with them. Sure – through the teenage years they stopped coming to see me every weekend, and my role in their lives changed. I played my part as a taxi driver to their own pursuits, whether it was to take Rebecca to her friend's house for a sleepover – or to drop Adam off at the pub. I was happy to be whatever they wanted. The one thing I always made sure of was that I was around. During the years I have had many opportunities to move away, to relocate back to Devon where my family live, but I have always hung around for them. I know that they appreciated me being around and I sure got a lot from seeing them grow up. I would have hated to have missed that part of their lives.

My ex-partner and I have always taken a relaxed attitude to the kids. We never fought about them and always communicated well about any issues relating to them. We did not always agree about the way they should be brought up – but that's just the way of the world. Although our relationship did not work, we did not get in each other's way after it finished.

Now, 15 years later, I have no contact with her. I have moved on in my life and have a new partner; the kids understand that my life is separate to their mother's and don't involve me in it. With three kids one of them is bound to tell me what (if anything) is affecting their mum, but for the most part we continue to live totally separate lives.

Having been a divorced dad and seen my children become adults I am glad that I stuck to my beliefs. Firstly that I would always be honest with the kids as this has helped me build a credible relationship with each of them. Secondly that I was always around for them even in their teenage years when they were busy doing other things (much more exciting than coming to see dad), and thirdly that I was their friend. This was especially important during the teenage years when they needed me to be more of a friend than an authority figure.

Communication was the key for me – being able to ask the kids for their opinion and getting their agreement has really helped me to be a good divorced dad. Now – 15 years later – I am thinking about moving to New Zealand. Having been there for them, all three of them want me to follow my own path.

Leaving bad feelings behind

Time enables both parents to move on with their lives, and the new direction that their lives take will help them to realise the futile nature of clinging on to hatred or vengeance from the past. In other words, what was important to them yesterday is not as important today or tomorrow. This will have an effect on how they treat each other – and on all the issues surrounding the kids.

A small percentage of divorced dads' ex-partners fail to change with time; they are so entrenched in their position that they fail to find a way to work with the dad for the benefit of the kids. In these circumstances – until the mum moves on – the dad will always find his relationship with his kids hampered by her efforts. However, the mum will pay a price because kids are not stupid, and as they get older – especially into their teenage years – they are able to decipher what is going on between their parents and arrive at their own conclusions. If their mum has been a barrier to them seeing their dad (and dad has always tried to be there), then she will get the full force of their wrath.

Of course some fathers fail to change with time and remain entrenched with the same problems and negative emotions that they felt during the separation. If this is the case then they will become increasingly bitter and twisted and it will be a barrier in their relationship with the kids.

Most divorced dads find that over time (maybe after a year or two) they become neutral about their ex-partner; they don't mind what she does with her life, and they find a way of being friendly towards her in front of the kids. This helps enormously as any conflict between the parents – even after separation – is a source of stress for the children.

Your ex is probably doing the same – she has probably realised that continuing to fight is not doing her any good (it is costing her money and energy) and is prepared to try a strategy of neutrality to give her an easier life. If she wanted to get back at you for the separation she may have had her revenge first and now, having felt that she has got even, she might be ready to accept a neutral stance for the sake of the kids. Whatever the reasons for the separation, time changes them as new events and fresh influences creep into people's lives.

Children and time

Time also has an effect on the children. If at the time of the separation the kids were not yet eight years old, then they will have been heavily influenced by their mum. But as they get older, and able to make their own decisions about who to spend time with and what to believe, they will have more of a say in their relationship with each parent. For this reason many divorced dads who stay the distance, even when they have to put up with manipulation and abuse from their ex, find that over time their relationship with their kids blossoms.

Time lets their kids make up their own minds about what happens. Time reduces any negative influence your ex has with the children. If the kids are older than eight, then the time when they will make their own decisions is even closer – and you only have to wait for a few years before your ex's influence is minimal.

Life changes

Time also has another influence. Life changes with time. It may be that you are faced with changes that bring fresh demands, and make having your relationship with your children even more difficult. Things such as:

◆ a new job;
◆ working away from home;
◆ a new partner (maybe even with her kids).

All these and other factors bring fresh demands on a divorced dad's time. What is important is that you always maintain space in your life for your children, even though this can be tested as your life changes and new demands for your time come along. You will need to manage your time throughout your children's upbringing.

8

Building your own support network

If you are going to cope through all the trials and tribulations of separation, then one of the things you need is a support network: a group of people you can turn to for advice, emotional support and practical assistance.

During the separation and the consequent battle for your rights, you will need a variety of support. This will be:

◆ financial
◆ emotional
◆ practical (eg a place to stay)
◆ advice on what to do next
◆ a shoulder to lean on
◆ a sympathetic ear
◆ a friend to give encouragement.

A network of friends and acquaintances to help you during this time makes the separation a lot easier to cope with. Men find it difficult to share their feelings and troubles with their friends and families. It is well-known (at least in the pub!) that women are more inclined to talk to their friends and family about their problems, whereas a bloke is more likely to bottle things up, and not open up to his mates. He should, because he would find a willing audience who may well themselves have been in that situation before and can offer some good advice.

YOUR FRIENDS

So instead of standing at the bar of your local, and telling your mates that you are OK, open up. When someone asks, 'How's it going?' tell the truth: 'Completely awful – I'm having some real problems with X'. Even if the person you are speaking to can't offer any advice, you will feel a hell of a lot better for getting things off your chest, and just the simple process of talking about matters will help.

Remember the old saying 'a problem shared is a problem halved'? Well, it might not be completely true – but then nor is the mantra 'a friend in need is a pain in the bum'. You might find that your mates respond well, even if it is to tell you that they know someone who had a similar problem, and maybe you can speak to them. Whatever the outcome, you will find that dealing with the problem on your own is not the best way to go about it. This is because you probably don't know what to do, and the only way of finding out, is to seek some support.

TIP
Don't bottle things up – create a network of people that can help you with your different needs at this time.

Of course you can always go to a solicitor for advice, but it will cost you money – an awful lot of money. And that may add to your financial problems. Clearly, you need to be able to lean on people who are going to act in your interests and be on your side; the best place to start is close to home.

The other reason you need friends around you is not necessarily to help with the issues of your divorce or separation, or to help out with the kids. But just to be around you, and help fill the social void that can be created when you leave a relationship. A lot of divorced dads find that they now have time on their hands to spend in other leisure pursuits – time you would have been doing simple things with your ex-partner or with the kids. A network of friends can help avoid becoming lonely or simply just sitting around doing nothing. If this is the case, make a fresh start – join a local football team or other activity to ensure that you don't sit around getting depressed.

YOUR FAMILY

Generally, family members are the best support that you can hope for. Whether it's your parents, or brothers and sisters (if they are old enough), these immediate family members can provide a raft of support. Clearly, unless they themselves have been separated, and in the position you are in, then they may have limited knowledge of how best to help. But families are the best source of aid in terms of emotional and physical support. You may need a place to stay whilst you are separating, you may need a place to bring the kids when you have access to them. Parents are also the best emotional support, as their love for you will help you feel good again, as well as ensuring that you have a shoulder to lean on.

Family members can also be used as a third party if you have to get messages to your ex-partner; you just need to make sure that the person you use is trusted by your ex. And families can help in loads of other ways:

♦ helping you to look after the kids when you have access;

♦ joining you on holidays with the kids to add to the fun;

♦ financially, they may be able to bridge a gap in your funds;

♦ providing someone to talk to – who cares about your situation.

CASE STUDY

Family support is important
Dad: Chris
Children: Claire aged 10, Mark aged five
Situation: Married for 13 years, divorced for 12 months

I knew that I was going to leave the family home probably a full year before I separated from my wife. Things were just going from bad to worse, and our relationship was over. However I loved my kids, and wanted to stay for as long as I could to protect them, because I knew that separation would be tough on them.

When I first moved out I was lucky – I was able to live for a short while with my brother who himself had been through a divorce a few years before. And as he had children too, he understood many of my concerns.

At first, communicating with my ex-wife was really tough. Every time I wanted to get things sorted she just referred back to the separation; I think she couldn't move forward because it was me who had chosen to leave and she did not accept it at first so the first few months were hard.

I made it clear to my kids that I had a new home, but she kept giving them confused messages about me coming back. My daughter did not really understand, and it caused my son real anguish. I just had to be resolute and I always told the children the truth.

Dealing with all the issues that hit me was really tough; I had to find a new home, to set divorce proceedings going as well as continue to pay for the family home. Within a short period of time I was skint. My ex-wife had some real concerns, mostly about the financial settlement, but once she was sure that I would not be difficult things got a bit easier.

The worst time for me during the first few months was dropping the kids back. Not only would my ex-wife try and pick a verbal fight with me (which I learned to avoid), but after spending time with them I often felt a bit low – it reminded me that life was changing, and that not being in the family home meant I couldn't rely on seeing the kids. I would have to always be making arrangements and doing things differently.

I thought long and hard about my approach to the children, what I would tell them and how I would be with them. A really good piece of advice was to always be positive about the situation, no matter how I felt. Even the times when my ex shouted at me in front of the kids I remained positive – I was determined not to let the kids know that I was uncomfortable with her treatment or that I did not expect things to go smoothly.

Having good advice was really valuable; my brother was able to tell me how to manage my anger when it all seemed a bit much, and the importance of being reasonable with my ex-wife. I am so glad that I did not lose it in front of the kids – not only did I not want the kids to have that image in their minds, I did not want to give my ex any ammunition against me.

Looking back at that time I realise that having good friends and some family around me at this time was really helpful. Simple things like knowing that I did not want to be on my own when I had seen the kids that day, or practical help, such as giving me a roof over my head. I often just rang them to have a talk about things. My family were great, really supporting me and rallied round.

Time moves on pretty quickly. Now I am happily divorced and set up in my own home, and most importantly the children have a new home as well as the old family one. They seem to be fine – in fact I would say that children are much more resilient than parents. Whatever the reason, I reckon that they were better at handling the upheaval than I was.

It is now 12 months later and I am just about back on my feet. My monthly income now matches my outgoings. The divorce settlement has come through, and I have been able to buy a house using funds from the settlement as a deposit. I think that I have done this in remarkably quick time – some of my friends have taken over three years to get their finances sorted. I had to comprise a lot (in fact I gave away more than I needed too), but getting it sorted quickly was definitely best for me, as I can now really get going on starting my new life.

If a mate of mine was to separate from his wife I would make sure that I was a really good friend and helped him through it – I don't mean with money, but with advice and encouragement. The best piece of advice I would give is to get it settled as quickly as possible, because then you can get on with building a new life.

OTHER ORGANISATIONS

Another area of support – one that is very important to a lot of divorced dads – is an organisation that will give you specific help in dealing with your situation. For many divorced dads this means joining an organisation such as Families Need Fathers.

Families Need Fathers

Many divorced dads feel that joining a support group or attending a meeting for dads is not an activity that they would consider. They think it sounds as if they are going along to the local branch of Alcoholics Anonymous, and have an idea it will be full of sad people who have lost their way and need help. Having to sit in a circle and say, 'My name is Bill, and I am a divorced dad who is having problems', is definitely the last thing that anybody wants to do.

But the truth is that joining Families Need fathers (FNF) is probably the best move you can make in getting real help and advice. This is because FNF is full of divorced dads who have been there, can tell you what your possible course of action is, and it costs you nothing more than a donation. For information about your local meeting, see the 'Useful Contacts' section at the back of the book.

Dave has attended several meetings, and says about the first time he went,

I felt great when I came out of the meeting because I discovered that there were other divorced dads who were in the same boat as me. My ex-partner had made allegations that were completely untrue, and my self-esteem was flattened. Simply hearing that I was not alone, and that this is a regular occurrence, made me feel as if I would be able to cope, and knowing that helped.

Chris, who has been attending meetings for a few months, agrees:

When I arrived at the meeting I thought that my situation would be the worst, and that there could not be another cow like my ex. But listening to the reports from the other divorced dads made me realise that I was not the worst man off in the room. And somehow, having sympathy for the others helped me.

Aims of Families Need Fathers
Below is an extract from the FNF's website (www.fnf.org.uk):

Families Need fathers is a registered UK charity which provides information and support to parents, including unmarried parents, of either sex. FNF is chiefly concerned with the problems of maintaining a child's relationship with both parents during and after family breakdown. Founded in 1974, FNF helps thousands of parents every year.

FNF receives no core funding and is reliant upon membership subscriptions and donations for its continued existence. The annual subscription costs less than a few minutes of a solicitor's time, and gives access to a wide range of information and support that is beyond the scope of some lawyers. We have a rapidly growing number of grandparents and women members.

What FNF believe

◆ *Children have a right to a continuing loving relationship with both parents.*

◆ *Children need to be protected from the harm of losing contact with one parent.*

◆ *Both parents should be treated equally and shared parenting should be encouraged.*

◆ *Each parent has a unique contribution to make to their children's development.*

◆ *The family courts should be backed by a nationally funded mediation service.*

◆ *Litigation is not the preferred route for resolving post separation children's matters.*

What FNF do

◆ *FNF work to increase awareness of the problems of family breakdown.*

◆ *FNF produce booklets, leaflets, a website and a regular newsletter.*

◆ *FNF hold local self-help branch meetings throughout the UK.*

◆ *FNF provide support to members through our internet forums.*

◆ *FNF operate a national helpline accredited by the Telephone Helplines Association.*

◆ *FNF have a network of volunteer telephone contacts.*

◆ *FNF run parenting support workshops.*

◆ *FNF provide speakers and case studies for the press and media.*

◆ *FNF participate in family policy forums and seminars.*

◆ *FNF respond to government consultations.*

◆ *FNF lobby Parliament and the legal profession.*

◆ *FNF collate and promote relevant research information.*

Fathers4Justice
Fathers4Justice was a dynamic movement with specific objectives and targets desperately needed to achieve for children and their families. Despite some good work, this organisation has now disbanded, and divorced dads don't have a clear national platform to promote changes in the law.

Other support organisations
The help and support that each dad needs varies. The important thing is that you do not attempt to handle it on your own, as assistance really can help in getting to the best solution for you and your children.

Other support organisations exist to help, covering all aspects of separation, divorce, and child welfare. The 'Useful Contacts' section at the back of the book has more details.

9

Paternity issues

Divorced dads can be faced with a whole series of issues to establish their right to be known as – and to act as – the father of their children. Establishing their paternity and dealing with their ex's attempts to change the name of their child are just two of the hurdles that some divorced dads have to cope with.

But other dads have been there before, which means that pretty much all the battles that you may have to fight have been fought before. So there are legal precedents set up which protect the rights of the child and the rights of the father. It may be difficult to fight for those rights, but they do exist in law. You just need to remember that getting justice can be a long and expensive exercise.

WHO'S THE DADDY?

If your name appears on your child's birth certificate, then many of your rights are protected by law. Although as you will discover, having a legal right does not necessarily mean that it will be automatically be respected. Fathers' rights are not always re-spected by mums; sometimes circumstances are against you.

There is whole set of problems for fathers whose relationships end before the kids are born. It may be that your name is not entered on the birth certificate. You *must* try to get your name on

255

it – your fundamental legal rights are affected by this one action. Without your name on the certificate you may find it much more difficult to get access and parental rights with your child. If you want to have a positive impact on your child's life you need to get your name on the birth certificate, or on a declaration of paternity (under the Family Law Act 1991).

THE LAW ON PATERNITY

The law on paternity can be complex. It is governed by the Family Law Act (1986), The Child Support Act (1991), The Children's Act (1989), and other acts which relate to parental interests.

If your ex-partner refuses to recognise you as the dad (either by agreeing to a declaration or by allowing your name to appear on the birth certificate) then your options are unfortunately limited. You will need to go through the process of establishing that you are indeed the father by means of DNA test.

The problem with this is the time and money it takes. To the ordinary man in the street, the legal and medical fees can be crippling. Dads that have been through this say that the process can take up to £20,000 and two years to complete. Of course, all the time this is happening you will probably not have any access to your child (and, to top it all, your ex-partner may be receiving on legal aid).

In these cases, the law errs on the side of caution, and will assume that you are not the real father. The principle of innocent until proven guilty does not translate to fathers. Yet again the law gives divorced dads second-rate treatment.

But you *can* do it, even though your ex has refused to acknowledge that you are the father. Even though it is a long battle, if you are indeed the father, then nothing can stop the inevitability of the legal decision going in your favour.

TIP

If you have a problem getting your ex-partner to recognise that you are the father, seek legal advice immediately, and get on with fighting for your rights through the courts.

When the mother's husband is not the child's father

There is a legal presumption that a child born to a married mother is a child of the marriage, and the husband (who may not be the father) has parental responsibility. A man who, for example, split up with his partner because he thought she was sleeping around, and is not the father of the children of the marriage, faces an uphill task in disproving it. Not only does he have to pay child maintenance (normally via the CSA) during the period that he is disproving it but also, following a recent court ruling on blood tests, the mum can refuse to comply with an order to obtain a blood test, and delay the matter for many years.

RIGHTS OF STEPDADS

Unfortunately you have no automatic right of access to any child unless you have parental rights. That is the short and unsavoury truth about second partners. Even though you may well go through the same set of emotions that a birth dad goes through when you separate from your step family, there is little that can be done legally.

In December 2005 there was a change in the law. The new Adoption and Children's Act 2002 came into force. Prior to the Act step parents had no legal recognition unless they had been to court and obtained parental responsibility, which is normally associated with a residency order. However, under the new legislation, this position was altered slightly and it was made easier for a step parent to obtain parental responsibility.

Now a step parent can with the consent of the parent(s) with parental responsibility be granted PR. If consent is not forthcoming then you can still apply to the court. But by allowing parent(s) with parental responsibility to make a simple deed, the law has increased the ability of a step parent to obtain parental responsibility.

If you have assumed the role of dad in a child's life, don't expect to be able to continue to have contact with that child if your relationship with mum breaks down. It may be that your ex is happy for you to continue to see the children. If so – great, but you must be aware that it may not last for ever. Your ex's life will be subject to changes as will yours. You may find other people enter your life, as they will probably enter the child's and mum's, and this may change perspectives and relationships.

It may be that mum wants you to be out of the children's life as quickly as she wants you out of hers. In which case there is little you can do about it. As a stepdad you have no automatic rights over your stepchildren – you need to obtain parental responsibility.

◆ Don't fight the impossible fight. If your ex does not want you to have parental responsibility or access to your stepchildren then you can't have it. You need to know when to concede a fight.

◆ Don't go hanging around the school or other places. You may well get a prohibited steps order placed against you, which will mean you have to spend time and money in a family court.

◆ Do try and persuade your ex that it is in the child's best interests to keep you in their life, and see what relationship can be built from there.

CHANGING A CHILD'S SURNAME

The law on changing a child's surname is very clear.

Prior to the implementation of the Children's Act 1989 in October 1991 the law governing the surname of the child was the Matrimonial Clause Act 1973, where:

On the certificate of satisfaction (for the divorce) for the arrange-ments for the children – that no one should take any action without the authority of the court which would result in the children being known by any other name.

The children of anyone divorcing before this date (October 1991) were automatically protected, and anyone taking action against this was in contempt of court.

The surname is also legally protected under the Children's Act 1989. Where a residency order is in place then Section 13-1 of the Act clearly applies:

Where a residency order is in force with respect to a child, no person may cause the child to be known by a new surname without the written consent of every person who has parental responsibility for the child or by the leave of the court.

This means is that if as part of your divorce a residency order was made for the children (or in cases prior to 1991 a certificate of satisfaction), there is no way that the mum can legally change the name of your children. At school, and on the child's legal documents (such as a passport) the name must be that of the father. Mum cannot simply make a change and have it stick.

TIP

Once a divorced dad has been given parental responsibility he *must* be consulted over any change of name by deed poll. That is the law.

There is, however, a problem for fathers who were not married, and where no residency order is in place. In these cases they must apply to the court for a prohibited steps order to stop their ex from making any changes to the surnames of their children. It is entirely possible for the mum not to put the father's name on the birth certificate.

If you were an unmarried father then there is another law that may also affect you. The Registration of Births and Deaths Act 1953 governs the registration of names – and where the father and mother are not married it is the duty of the mother to register the birth within 42 days. Section 10–1 prohibits the registrar from entering the father's name on the birth certificate without the co-operation and consent of the mum (unless there is a court order in force) and whilst Section 10 allows a re-registration, applying the father's name, it is only done with the mother's consent. Hence, it is not a legal requirement for a mother to state the name of the father when registering the child, so it may be quite a legal fight for the dad to have his child carry his name.

10

Parent Alienation Syndrom (or Implacably Hostile Parent)

Many divorced dads get the feeling that their ex is opposed to their contact. Not that this manifests itself in an obvious manner. Mum will sit opposite a judge and seem as natural as can be, but all the time she is placing a series of blocks in his way – often using the children themselves as an excuse to stop contact. But implacably hostile mums are trying to turn the child against the father. This is becoming increasingly prevalent, not just here in the UK.

This phenomenon has been studied in depth in the USA and is called Parent Alienation Syndrome. Dr R Gardner started studying it as early as 1987, and it is now recognised by the courts as a major problem in child custody cases. The term Parent Alienation Syndrome is being picked up here in the UK although in our courts it is more commonly known as 'implacably hostile to contact'. But it is one and the same thing.

Parent Alienation Syndrome is dramatic, very harmful to the children and can manifest itself in many ways. A frequent example is where the mother appears in principle to support contact completely, but the child expresses anxiety or even fear at the idea of contact. Although the court welfare officer talking to this child may suspect that the mother is the real obstacle to contact, and that she has coached the child, nevertheless it appears that the child is expressing genuine views.

Parental alienation is where there is a singular relationship between a child and one parent, to the exclusion of the other parent. The fully alienated child is a child who does not wish to have any contact whatsoever with one parent and who expresses only negative feelings for that parent and only positive feelings for the other parent. This child has lost the range of feelings for both parents that is normal for a child.

There is a range of levels of severity manifested by mum (or sometimes dad). This means that there is a range of effects that the alienation will have – not only on the relationship that child has with both the parents – but also on the child's longer-term social and emotional wellbeing. The alienation process is believed to set up conditions that interfere with the quality of the relationship with the alienated parent, which in turn adds to maladjustment in the child.

Given that at a significant number of divorcing couples face intense conflict over contact issues, the potential is fairly large for the undercurrents of tension and conflict to produce conditions in which divorced dads report alienation concerns to their solicitor or at court. In other words, if your ex-partner is really angry with you, she may well try to turn the kids against you.

For a lot of mums it is temporary, and when their anger subsides normality returns. However for some mums this is not the case, and as a result of conflict either from the separation, or from subsequent acts, she adopts a position where she starts to alienate the children against the father.

Degrees of hostility (alienation)

Varying degrees of alienation have been described, ranging from mild to severe.

In the most severe cases, the mothers are often seen as fanatical, using everything possible to prevent contact. They will often insist on CAFCASS reports, on welfare visits, on protracted mediation. They will produce last-minutes issues and problems which get in the way of progress, as well as expressing views of dissatisfaction about the court and its process.

They are obsessed with antagonism toward the father, and will behave in a way that is a clear and consistent derogation of him. Some cases involve a combination of brainwashing and hostility that begins with the alienating parent and is taken on by the alienating child. So mums actually believe the tales that they are telling, and then brainwash both themselves and others around them (including the children) into believing it. If your separation was as a result of any issues of abandonment and betrayal it will help to fuel and prolong this anger.

In moderate cases the mother appears less fanatical but still quite enraged. These mothers are quite angry and often vengeful in their behaviour toward the other parent. They feel hurt, and expect the child to take sides and be loyal to them over their relationship with the other parent. Moderate alienating parents will work very hard to prevent contact and to interfere with the quality of the relationship between the father and the child. They are unreceptive to complying with court orders but will do so minimally to avoid negative legal consequences.

They may bring up sexual abuse allegations, but they can differentiate between preposterous claims and the more plausible. They seem to delight in hearing negative news about the dad and they communicate their dislike of contact or access arrangements. They often refuse to speak to the other parent and may make derogatory remarks about them to the child. They will hold fast to their view of needing to protect the children from this other parent and see the other parent as untrustworthy, yet appear more subtle in their expression of these views with the child, friends, or CAFCASS officer.

Finally, mild cases of parental alienation tend to be more focused and limited in scope. Dr Gardner has suggested that these mothers have a healthier bond with the children and are able to recognise that alienation from the father is not in the best interests of the child. They are more willing to take a conciliatory approach to the father's requests.

They may still have little regard for the importance of contact or access and tend to have difficulty tolerating the presence of the other parent at events important to the child. These milder cases involve subtle attempts at turning the child against the other parent and drawing the child into the alienating parent's view-point. This may involve conscious and unconscious actions. The main motive may be for the parent to look better in the eyes of the child.

The effects on the father are simple. In the worst cases he does not get to see his children, and has to spend years fighting through the courts (where PAS is not yet recognised as a real and growing problem). In less severe cases, he has to put up with contact abuse and lesser contact with his children than he would like, and less than is good for the child.

But the real problem with parent alienation is the long-term effects it will have on the children.

Long-term effects of parent alienation on the child

As well as the harmful effects on the relationship with the father, and the damage that this can do to the relationship with the mother, there are other significant worries. According to Dr Gardner's study, long-term effects of alienation, if left unchecked, may lead to various pathological symptoms in the child, which may not manifest themselves until they grow up to become an adult. These include:

- splitting in their relationships

- difficulties in forming intimate relationships

- a lack of ability to tolerate anger or hostility in relationships

- psychosomatic symptoms and sleep or eating disorders

- psychological vulnerability and dependency

- conflicts with authority figures

- an unhealthy sense of entitlement for one's rage that leads to social alienation in general.

How can you tell if your ex is alienated?

Just looking at the mum's attitude to the father does not tell the full story. If she is determined to alienate the child from the dad she may go a lot further than you might expect. This is because she has to back up or justify her actions and will try to get others to back her views, even if they are not in the best position to represent the views of the child.

Alienation in its true form is not just a few weeks of aggro. It is the establishment of a long-term position of the mother (and hence the children) against the father. Most divorced dads will at some point have to face an ex who is p***ed off with them, and telling the kids things that are not helpful. But this is not alienation, it is simply venting frustration. It becomes alienation when she tries to change the attitude of the child against the dad in the longer term.

The results of this may be some, or all, of the following:

1. The views expressed by the child (for example, 'I'm frightened of daddy', or 'I hate daddy') are not in any way borne out by the child's behaviour when observed by other people.
2. The mother 'enmeshes' others (who may become her witnesses) who then echo the child's fear or allegations and support the mother's view that contact can only begin very gradually.
3. The mother is reluctant to allow the child to be seen by independent psychologists although she may have enlisted the support of her general practitioner.
4. The mother agrees to arrangements for contact and at the last moment 'pulls the plug', often citing a real or imagined incident whereby the father has upset the children.
5. The mother is monitoring or trying to interrupt telephone contact between the children.
6. The child checks with mother (which may merely be by using

body language) that it is all right to answer questions asked by social workers or experts in the mother's presence.

7. The child does not answer questions naturally, but appears instead to give pre-programmed answers, or responds to a question by giving a wholly unrelated answer; a classic case of indoctrination.

8. The mother insists on being present at all contact sessions, citing the child's need to feel secure, or the mother may say that the child has told her that they are too frightened to have contact unless she stays.

9. It is said that letters and cards from the father mysteriously fail to arrive, although the mother encourages the child to write so as to demonstrate the commitment to contact.

10. Immediately after contact, the mother asks the child how they are feeling (for example 'have you still got that nasty tummy ache?'), implying that contact has been a painful experience for the child.

11. The mother alleges that the father has abused the child in some way, and continues to insist on this even in the face of all expert evidence to the contrary. None the less, the mother may assure everyone that she does not want to prohibit contact but insists that it will have to be re-established on a very gradual step-by-step basis and that continued supervision of the father whilst contact takes place is essential to prevent further abuse. The child may echo the allegations of the mother, appearing to believe that they have been abused.

However Parent Alienation is shown by the mum, the result is twofold. Firstly that she is trying to persuade the CAFCASS officer or other court officials to stop or curtail contact because it is not in the best interest of the child. Secondly, she is trying to alienate the child against having contact with their father for no good reason other than her own motives.

What to do if this sounds like your ex-partner

God help any divorced dads whose ex-partner is becoming so hostile that they can be deemed to be acting in an implacably hostile way. In many UK court rooms this syndrome is not understood enough or even recognised by the judges and many solicitors do not have an understanding of how to use it as a legal argument. There is currently no real attempt for the courts to identify the stages of PAS that a parent is subjecting her child to – and no attempt for a court to remedy it. In addition, CAFCASS is very unwilling to lose its neutral status and make a judgement that mum is harming the child because of PAS.

PAS remains a vile problem for a small percentage of divorced dads, whose relationship with their children will never be able to recover from the damage that PAS does. What is clear is that no solution will be available in the short term, because it will take a great deal of time for the law to change and recognise this as a problem which affects children.

If you choose to walk away you will be giving your ex exactly what she wants, and unlike other cases where a break in the battle enables both parents to reassess their positions and think about the best for the child, mums who are under the influence of PAS will see a break in your contact or legal fight as a victory to be built on. They will see a break in your attempts at contact as a vindication of their actions.

The only advice that can be given is to hang on in there, to minimise your costs of fighting through the courts, and to hope that one day you will get to re-establish a relationship with your children. You could keep a diary and record what goes on – in the future it may help your children understand what you've had to go through in your battle to have a meaningful relationship with them.

Look for other divorced dads in the same position, and try and get as many hints and tips from them about how best to cope with what you have to face.

CASE STUDY

Parent Alienation Syndrome
Dad: Martin
Child: Amy (age one when separated)
Situation: Lived with ex-partner (never married)

I left my ex-partner because I was having an affair. Since that day, over four years ago, I have rarely seen my daughter. I have been to court in excess of 19 times, and had three CAFCASS reports, each clearly stating that there is no reason why I should not have unsupervised access to Amy. My ex still refuses to co-operate with any court action or communicate with me.

Since the day I left my ex life has been great, but a piece of it has been missing: my daughter. I expected my ex-partner to be angry with me for a while but I never expected her to try and expunge me from my daughter's life as a way of getting back at me. I did not realise the pure hatred that my ex would have for me, and the extent to which she would go to remove me from my own daughter's life.

For the first three years of the court action I was not even allowed to have my daughter call me dad. This hurt like you can't believe, especially since my ex, who had found another partner, got my daughter to call him dad. That relationship has now finished. My daughter, who has been calling another man 'dad' for the last three years, has (in the court's opinion) been emotionally damaged by her mum's attitude to her real father. It took three years and a court order specifying that my ex-partner had to tell my daughter who her father was to sort it out.

Over the years my ex has been forced by the court to go to mediation. As a result of the CAFCASS reports the court has even appointed my daughter her own solicitor. During this time I have been able to see her for a few short hours at a contact centre. Every effort the court has made to get my ex-partner to allow me to pick her up from the family home has, as yet, failed. I have since got remarried and have another daughter. To this day my ex has not allowed Amy to meet her half sister, or come around to my new home.

My ex-partner never fails to accept my child maintenance payments each month but refuses to let me see her.

I don't know what drives my ex-partner. It's not as if she hasn't already moved on in her life, but she seems to be typical of those mums who suffer from Parent Alienation Syndrome. She is completely hostile to any form of contact arrangement. She genuinely believes that Amy is better off with a singular parent to the exclusion of dad – and certainly cannot see any benefit for Amy in developing a relationship with her half sister.

The CAFCASS officer was useless – he seemed to always want my ex to co-operate with the courts. I think that he completely failed to understand that she was actually hostile to contact with me. He wrote report after report telling the court that I was a good parent. But he refused to tell the judge to make a definitive order as he always hoped that my ex's attitude would change.

Of course we are still waiting, and I am still waiting to get unsupervised access to Amy.

Given my ex's parental alienation, I know that my efforts to get to see my daughter will fail. My ex will ignore any order that the judge makes, and the law (as it stands) cannot be enforced. I have resigned myself to the fact that I will probably not get to develop a relationship with my daughter, certainly whilst her mum's attitude to me remains the way it does. Amy will be negatively influenced against me, irrespective of court orders or action; my ex will poison her attitude towards me, despite my best efforts to be a loving dad.

But I will never give up. I am resolved to always attempt to see her – it does not matter to me how many times I have to stand in front of a judge and I don't care how many CAFCASS reports I have to subject myself to. I will never give up trying. I know that at some point in the future (even if it is 15 years away) Amy will start to communicate with me, away from her mother's alienation.

When she does I will show her the huge filing cabinet full of court papers; I will show her the evidence that I always wanted to be her dad. I have kept each and every court report which details my efforts to see her, and clearly shows her mother being told by the courts to let her see her dad. These papers stand over two feet high, and I will be able to show her that I never gave up, that I always obeyed the law, always wanted to be involved in her life, and most importantly, that many judges, social workers, and even a court-appointed guardian wanted her to have a dad.

It was only her mum who thought otherwise; it was only her implacably hostile attitude toward me that was the problem. I will then let her decide if she wants to start to see me, and if she does then I will want to do what I can to be her proper dad.

Useful contacts

CAFCASS
www.cafcass.gov.uk
020 7510 7000

Childline
www.childline.org.uk
0800 1111

Children's Legal Centre
www.childrenslegalcentre.com
01206 873820

CSA
www.csa.gov.uk

Community Legal Service Direct
www.justask.org.uk

Families Need Fathers
www.fnf.org.uk
020 7613 5060

Gingerbread for lone parents and children
www.gingerbread.org.uk
0800 0184318

Grandparents Federation
www.grandparents-association.org.uk
01279 444964

National Association of Child Contact Centres
www.naccc.org.uk
0845 4500 280

National Council for One-Parent Families
www.oneparentfamilies.org.uk
0800 018 5026

NCH Family Mediation and Support Services
www.itsnotyourfault.org/nchmediation.html

National Family Mediation
www.nfm.u-net.com
01392 271610

National Family & Parenting Institute
www.e-parents.org
020 7424 3460

NSPCC
www.nspcc.org.uk
0800 8005000

Parentline
www.parentlineplus.org.uk
0808 800 2222

Samaritans
www.samaritans.org.uk
0845 5990

Index